PRAISE FOR

Why Can't You Read My Mind?

"Thank you for giving us such a practical and eloquent book on how to permanently improve our intimate relationships! All couples should read this book and give their relationship a chance for a deeper and longer lasting love."

—*Nadine J. Carpenter, LCSW*

"This book speaks to what you can do to help your relationship become better, less conflicted, and more romantic—even if your partner doesn't read it!"

Steven D. Mullinix, Ph.D.

"In a single source, Bernstein and Magee have assembled a set of 'cognitive tools' that will assist any motivated couple in making meaningful changes in their relationship. I recommend this book not only to individuals struggling with relationship difficulties, but also to beginning counselors who want to increase the specificity of their cognitive techniques in marital counseling."

—*Monroe A. Bruch, Professor of Counseling Psychology, University of Albany, State University of New York*

ABOUT THE AUTHORS

JEFFREY BERNSTEIN, PH.D., is a licensed psychologist specializing in family and couples therapy in the Philadelphia area. With over fifteen years of clinical experience, he has treated hundreds of couples, families, and individuals. Dr. Bernstein has also given numerous workshops and seminars on relationship issues. Using his powerful discoveries about the toxic thinking problem in intimate relationships, he has helped many couples on the brink of separation and divorce think their way back to love.

SUSAN MAGEE is an award-winning writer of fiction and nonfiction and coauthor of several books, including *The Power of Positive Confrontation* and *When the Little Things Count*. Magee lives with her family outside Philadelphia.

WHY, Can't YOU Read MY Mind?

JEFFREY BERNSTEIN, PH.D.
& Susan Magee

WHY
Can't
YOU
Read
MY
Mind?

Overcoming the 9
Toxic Thought Patterns
That Get in the Way
of a Loving Relationship

Da Capo
LIFE
LONG

A MEMBER OF THE PERSEUS BOOKS GROUP

Copyright © 2004 by Jeffrey Bernstein and Susan Magee

All rights reserved. No part of this publication may
be reproduced, stored in a retrieval system, or transmitted, in any
form or by any means, electronic, mechanical, photocopying, recording,
or otherwise, without the prior written permission of the publisher.
Printed in the United States of America. For information, address
Da Capo Press, 11 Cambridge Center, Cambridge, MA 02142.
Designed by Pauline Neuwirth, Neuwirth & Associates, Inc.
Set in 10.5 point ACaslon by the Perseus Books Group

Cataloging-in-Publication data for this book is available
from the Library of Congress.

ISBN-13: 978-1-56924-475-3

Published by Da Capo Press
A Member of the Perseus Books Group
www.dacapopress.com
Note: The information in this book is true and complete to the
best of our knowledge. This book is intended only as an informative guide
for those wishing to know more about health issues. In no way is this book
intended to replace, countermand, or conflict with the advice given to you by your
own physician. The ultimate decision concerning care should be made between
you and your doctor. We strongly recommend you follow his or her advice.
Information in this book is general and is offered with no guarantees on the
part of the authors or Da Capo Press. The authors and publisher disclaim all
liability in connection with the use of this book. The names and identifying
details of people associated with events described in this book have been
changed. Any similarity to actual persons is coincidental.

Da Capo Press books are available at special discounts for bulk purchases
in the U.S. by corporations, institutions, and other organizations. For more
information, please contact the Special Markets Department at the Perseus
Books Group, 2300 Chestnut Street, Suite 200, Philadelphia, PA, 19103,
or call (800) 255-1514, or e-mail special.markets@perseusbooks.com.

25 24 23 22 21 20 19

To my children, Alissa, Sam, and Gabby for all the joy you bring to me. You mean so much to me and I'm very proud of all three of you. I love you all very much.

To my parents, Evelyn and Lou, for being so supportive, loving, and encouraging to me throughout my life.

To Ralph and Tony for your invaluable gift of friendship. You are both great guys.

J.B.

To my boys, Dave and Christopher

S.M.

CONTENTS

INTRODUCTION

Whatever Happened to Happily Ever After?

WE ALL KNOW that relationships are not easy. We know in our heads that our partners aren't mind readers. Yet "Why doesn't he get it?" or "If she only didn't nag me" are just two of the many common complaints that express the frustration of dissatisfied people in intimate relationships.

It seems that everywhere we turn, we see and hear about people who are unhappy because they feel that something is missing in their intimate relationships. We overhear complaints about relationships in grocery store lines, restaurants, waiting rooms, and even at the dry cleaners ("He's so picky, he even likes his polo shirts dry cleaned").

Once, on a warm beautiful day, I climbed Squaw Peak in Arizona. There I was, getting directly in touch with Mother Nature, hiking up this scenic mountain, when, to my astonishment, I heard some passing hikers complaining about their spouses and significant others! There's no escaping relationship angst—even in the wilderness.

When it comes down to it, we just want to feel loved, understood, accepted, and appreciated. Naturally, we look to our intimate relationships to meet these needs, but more and more often we end up feeling disappointed and let down. So many people are going about life like the "walking wounded" because they don't feel fulfilled by their intimate relationships.

If you're reading this book, I assume that you too feel like one of the walking wounded—at least from time to time. Maybe you wish your partner knew what to say, what to do, and how to react to you in ways that really worked. Or maybe you just wish your partner could better meet your needs, stop being a jerk, understand you a little bit better, or give up some bad habits.

Have you ever thought that if you could change just one incredibly annoying thing about your significant other you'd finally be happy?

And if you really are soul mates, why *can't* he or she read your mind?

If you think even just one of the above, you are not alone. In fact, it's a little scary and even sad how much company you have. Thousands of couples—whether married, remarried, living together, dating, same-sex, young, or old—are fed up, unhappy, frustrated, disgusted, or just plain worn out from trying to make their relationships work. Thousands more are trying to figure out the secret to a lasting and successful relationship. Tragically, thousands and thousands of couples are so fed up and worn out that they're not only about to throw in the relationship towel, they're being strangled by it.

MANY RELATIONSHIPS ARE DOOMED

IT'S SAD BUT true—many relationships are doomed from the start. All too often, communication between couples breaks down. Partners fail to meet each other's needs. The worst part is that in the beginning, those happy couples full of hope weren't just kidding themselves. They really did think that they would make it, beat the odds, and live through the rest of their lives together, smiling, for the most part, hand in hand.

So what happens to us in relationships that kills our wonderful intentions? Why is it that so many of us, despite our best intentions and our highest hopes, can't seem to keep our relationships healthy, or even keep them alive at all? With all the talk shows and best-selling books about how to have a successful relationship, why do so many relationships still turn into a big, ugly mess? Why do so many of us eventually give up and break up, separate, or divorce?

Couples have given me many explanations for why their relationships have failed. There's the classic "We just drifted apart." I can't tell you how any times I've heard that one! Wood drifts apart—people don't. Unresolved issues and communication problems cause distance between people in a relationship. When you say, "We just drifted apart," what you really mean is, "We don't love each other anymore" or "We don't have the same feelings for each other anymore."

Or how about this one: "She/He turned out to be nuts." Sorry, this reason just doesn't cut it either. We're all weird and strange to some degree; there are very few saints and angels left in the world.

I also hear "We really don't have much in common" quite often. Hmmm . . . then why is it that you got together in the first place? And why is it that so many couples have different interests and yet are happy together?

Another reason for splitting up is "We fight too much." To this I say it isn't about *how much* you fight, but rather *how* you fight. You'll learn a lot about fighting fair in Chapter Nine.

Possibly the most threatening and damaging explanation for why a relationship fails is "I have fallen in love with someone else." A new romantic involvement or relationship brings all the energy, passion, fun, and sense of validation that your current relationship may have lost. Many people misinterpret this external fantasy partner as a true love, only to realize later that the inevitable pressures and disappointments of life tarnish the image of their newfound, shining soul mate. Sadly, their "gem" usually turns out to be nothing more than fool's gold.

WHY HAPPILY EVER AFTER IS REALLY SO HARD

SEVERAL YEARS AGO, I began to notice that there were common roadblocks to communication and intimacy, common themes of struggle and misunderstanding on which almost every couple who came to me for help got stuck. I kept hearing statements like "It's her fault," "He never listens," "She should know that I hate that," "His problem is that he is just a selfish person," and "I just can never please her."

Then, during a session one day, a woman threw up her hands in disgust, pointed at her husband, and shouted, "After all these years, you should know how I hate that!"

He shouted back, "How—how am I supposed to know? What am I, a mind reader?".

Wham! This couple's words struck me with a bolt of insight. I realized that they had verbalized a basic, underlying belief that all of my clients shared—that their partners were out to deprive them or drive them crazy. The faces of past couples flashed before me and each partner's desperate pleas to feel understood by the other echoed in my head. All of these couples were making the same misguided and frustrated plea: *Why can't you just get it? You never understand me! WHY CAN'T YOU READ MY MIND?".*

Their words—negative, presumptuous, and often destructive—came directly from the inaccurate, distorted thoughts and beliefs that each partner had about the other—that he should know I need a hug, that she had no right to gain weight after I married her, that he never listens. Instead of accepting their partners as real people with their own opinions, beliefs, and experiences, my clients wanted their partners to be transformed into mind readers, flawless soul mates, and miracle workers devoid of their own imperfections and hang-ups.

At first, many of the couples I counseled didn't want to accept this revelation. They were convinced it all came down to one problem. "But she/he really doesn't listen to me," they'd say.

I know in the heat of the moment people really believe that they are telling me the truth: "He really doesn't listen," "She always talks too much," "He's inconsiderate beyond belief". . . . Such distorted thoughts shine like beacons in the sea of frustration in which people in poor, problematic relationships feel they are drowning. But hold on; think about it. It's virtually impossible that your partner never listens to you or never performs a considerate act. It may honestly seem that way to you at times, but I have yet to meet a person who never listens or who is incapable of being considerate. Of course, when one partner accuses the other of "never listening," the other partner reacts and sends the couple on a whole new tangent that usually goes something like this: "That's not true. Just last night I listened to you for two hours . . ." or "Well, how about what you did . . .".

I don't know any mind readers. I also don't know any blameless people. I don't know anyone who can handle being told "You're nuts!" or "You're the worst nag" or "I have never met anyone as difficult as you!". Yet these were the kinds of toxic thoughts being verbalized in my office, as if there wasn't a doubt in the world that they were true. And, the emotional damage resulting from these toxic thoughts was huge.

I found that unless I could get couples to stop and address these toxic distortions, I was no better than a referee calling time-outs and sending people to the sidelines. I even considered buying a whistle—it was that bad. There could be no forward motion, no progress, unless these couples were able to stop, recognize what was keeping them stuck, and free themselves from these destructive thoughts. I realized that if couples could get over their toxic thinking toward each other, a tremendous obstacle to communication, empathy, trust, and all the other makings of a good relationship was suddenly removed. Only then were they in a position to work through their problems together.

Eventually, I discovered that there were nine specific types of relationship-sabotaging, destructive thoughts that repeatedly emerged. Some couples had three different toxic thought patterns at work in their relationship, others had six or seven, but one thing was for sure, every couple had at least one. This book will teach you how to break all nine of these toxic thought patterns and restore healthy and balanced thinking about your partner and your relationship.

A COMMON, YET UNDERRECOGNIZED PROBLEM

ONCE I TUNED into this problem, even recognizing it in myself, I began to look for books in the literature of cognitive therapy (a form of psychotherapy that teaches how certain flawed and problematic ways of thinking result in feelings of unhappiness, stress, anxiety, or depression by giving you a distorted picture of your life) to deepen my own understanding of this problem. I had been inventing techniques to help couples "detoxify," but I wanted to do so much more. After a long search, I discovered, to my disappointment, that there was virtually no information available or attention given to this extremely common and damaging relationship problem. Some books briefly mentioned that our "negative beliefs" or "problem attitudes" about our partners can be harmful to relationships, but such beliefs or attitudes were only vaguely touched upon. My clients and I felt that the one or two books I did find that covered the subject in somewhat more detail were overly technical and not reader-friendly, with the key information about this phenomena buried under a mountain of other advice about communication, conflict resolution, and gender differences. It's hard to believe, but the devastating impact of toxic thoughts on intimate relationships has, to a large extent, been sorely neglected and ignored. This omission has left couples unaware and unarmed with the knowledge they need to deal with the damage from their toxic thoughts.

Unfortunately, most people are unaware that they even *have* toxic thoughts, let alone that such thoughts damage their relationships. It also concerns me that many relationship counselors are largely oblivious to the impact of toxic thoughts on couples. Expecting to save and enhance your relationship without fixing your toxic thinking problems is like building a house on quicksand—the only place you are going is down!

CONFESSIONS OF A FORMER TOXIC THINKER

I AM NOT someone who is generally prone to toxic thinking—anymore. In general, I think I'm a pretty positive, rational guy—now. I like getting up in the morning. I am in a satisfying, fulfilling relationship. I love my children. I love my work. I have great, supportive friends. In fact, you would think that someone in my role as a therapist, someone whose job is to point out toxic thinking to others, someone writing a book about toxic thinking, would be completely free from such thoughts.

Well guess what? The more I worked with couples in crisis the more I discovered that toxic thinking was the common denominator for most of them—*and* for me. When it came to problems in my own intimate relationships, I discovered an unpleasant truth about myself:

I was a toxic thinker. In past relationships, I would suddenly find myself reacting strongly to actions or statements from my partners, but I had great difficulty determining why I reacted so strongly. Now I know that I had toxic thoughts about my partners. So often, unless we are made aware of our toxic thinking patterns in our relationships, we will move from one partner to another and repeatedly suffer emotional injury as a result of our toxic thinking.

Unfortunately, my ten-year marriage fell prey to toxic thinking. Looking back, though, I am grateful for what I learned from the pain that I experienced. I am also grateful for what I've learned from working with so many couples besieged with problems that have been created, in large part, by their toxic thinking. I have put these insights and strategies into this book. I share with you their struggles and their stories (though not their real names), and I offer you a surprisingly simple way to extinguish the toxic thoughts that destroy relationships.

HOW THIS BOOK CAN HELP YOU

THE FIRST PART of this book defines toxic thinking and explains how it destroys intimacy, trust, empathy, and romance—in other words, why "happily ever after" is so hard to find. The second part of this book gives you an easy-to-implement plan to break the vicious cycle of toxic thinking in your relationship. As you'll discover, this three-step approach (which I call MAP) can help you have a happier, more satisfying relationship. I also give you many tools for rebuilding empathy, repairing communication, learning how to resolve your conflicts, and finding real romance—all the elements of a healthy relationship that get squashed under the weight of toxic thinking.

Other areas of your life will improve, too. My clients tell me that by freeing themselves from the crippling shackles of toxic thinking, they not only feel better about their partners, they feel better about their relationships with coworkers and friends. And, best of all, they feel better about themselves. Why? Because people who suffer from toxic thinking don't just have relationship problems, they have self-esteem and confidence issues as well.

I hope that if you're dissatisfied with your relationship, you don't give up on it until you've read this book. I hope you don't give up on the belief that you can have a satisfying, lasting, and happy relationship. I've helped hundreds of couples restore love to their relationships with the advice and information in these pages. I promise you, the techniques you will find here can help you save your relationship and even help you significantly improve other areas of your life.

You can do this! You can save or improve your relationship. And even if you're not in a relationship right this minute, but have had frustrating relationships in the past, this book can help you. It might even transform your life.

Yes, really! Stick with me. You'll soon learn what toxic thinking is and how you can stop it from interfering with your happiness and satisfaction with your relationship.

1

A Happier Relationship Is All in Your Head

So what is the real secret to having a happy and loving relationship? I'm going to give you the answer and you will probably be surprised at it, but first you need to ask yourself one question: What do happy, satisfied couples have that I don't have?

You may be thinking that happy, satisfied couples know how to maintain a stronger sense of commitment than you do. Okay, maybe they do, but why? You may say that couples with smiling faces know how to communicate more effectively. That may be true as well, but why is that?

Why is it that happy couples know how to fight more effectively and resolve conflicts? And why is it that some couples endure, still hold hands, stay close to one another, and appear to have something you never had or can't find anymore—romance?

The secret you've been searching for, the key to finally ridding

A Happier Relationship Is All in Your Head   9

yourself of the frustration, anger, disappointment, and hidden resentments that drive you to the breaking point, that force you to ask, "Should I stay or should I get out of this?" is already within you.

That's right, *you*. All you need to do is turn to yourself—not your partner. I know this is hard because we've all been conditioned to think that another person is supposed to make us happy. So many of us have been duped into thinking that if he just changed this one thing, or if she could just get a grip about _____ (fill in the blank), then we would *finally be happy*.

Can you imagine how great life could be if you were no longer weighed down by dissatisfaction with and angst about your relationship? Well, I've got some really good news for you: There is a very strong chance that your relationship can be much more satisfying, fulfilling, and loving. But you must stop passively fantasizing that your partner is going to wake up one day, read your mind, and magically find a way to make you happy. Instead of being so fixated on what is (or is not) going on in your partner's mind, you need to become very aware of what is happening in your own head. Before you throw down this book and say, "But you don't understand, it really *is* my partner who is causing the problems," let me show you how much influence and control *you* have over your relationship happiness by teaching you to better read your own mind—not your partner's.

I agree that happy, satisfied couples, the ones who beat the odds and don't split up, break up, divorce, or simply stick it out for the sake of the kids, do tend to have strong commitment to each other and effective communication. They are able to fight fairly and resolve conflicts. They know how to be romantic.

But that's not all they have in common.

What happy couples have above and beyond anything else is a better, more realistic, and healthier way of thinking about each other. (And I don't just mean thinking things like *He's such a good guy*, or *Wow, I'm so in love with her*.) It is this better way of thinking that enables these couples to improve communication, solve problems, and enhance romance. This better way of thinking, this true foundation for a happy relationship, this elusive secret to your relationship success can be found in one place and one place alone—inside your own mind.

The couples I've worked with over the last fifteen years who have been able to recognize and stop a pervasive yet hidden and little-known relationship problem I call toxic thinking are the couples who make it. These are the couples who remain, against the odds, a unified force, still together and making it work. These are the couples about whom I, with great conviction, think, *Well, if anyone has a chance at lasting happiness, they do.*

Now you do, too.

WHAT EXACTLY IS TOXIC THINKING?

IN ORDER TO understand what toxic thinking is and how, like a cancer, it eats away at the bonds of trust and intimacy until a relationship collapses, you must first understand what you do inside your head all day, every single day of your life: you "self-talk."

Okay, so what is self-talk?

You know those silent conversations you have with yourself throughout the day? Conversations like *I have to go to the grocery store and pick up eggs. But I'm so tired. Why do I always get stuck in traffic?*

That's self-talk. Occasionally, you may catch yourself talking out loud or mumbling to yourself during these internal dialogues. That's self-talk, too. Whether you eventually verbalize these thoughts or not, they are the private conversations you have with yourself day in and day out.

We all self-talk—in the shower, waiting in line at the bank, staring at your computer screen, or having lunch with friends. We often self-talk without even realizing that we're doing it. Self-talk is really just another habit you've formed over years and years of thinking. It's like we have these internal tapes that repeatedly play themselves and, unless we make ourselves consciously aware of what they're saying, they just keep playing and we unconsciously digest the information.

Self-talk—even when we aren't aware of the contents—is perfectly normal and healthy, even if it's occasionally negative. Occasional negative thoughts, though they may be unpleasant, are normal. When you feel down or blue, you may say some negative things to yourself, such as *Dating is really hard for me.* That's normal.

WHEN THOUGHTS TURN TOXIC

YOUR THOUGHTS GET you into trouble, however, when the negative ones stop being occasional and become more frequent, habit-like, unrealistic, intense, and distorted. When that happens, you're experiencing toxic thinking.

We all think occasional negative thoughts, such as *I wish I were more careful, I did not really do a good job listening to him,* or *I don't like how I look after gaining this weight.* In many cases, negative self-talk, though it does not leave you feeling elated, can have some truth behind it. Maybe you really could have been more careful, or listened more effectively, and maybe you would look more attractive if you lost the weight you gained.

As the box on page 14 illustrates, there is a continuum of thought from positive to toxic. Toxic thoughts are negative thoughts that have lost their basis in reality and have gotten out of control, causing you to lose your perspective. Toxic thoughts, as you will see, are more extreme versions of negative thoughts. Unlike a negative thought like *I don't like how I look,* toxic thoughts are twisted, distorted, highly negative perceptions that are simply not based in reality, like *I'm ugly, No one finds me attractive,* or *I'll always be fat.*

In the upcoming chapters, I am going to show you how to conquer your toxic thoughts, not simply transform you into a positive thinker. As you can see from the box below, positive thoughts are included in the range of thinking options we have. But hang on! Just saying, "Okay, so all I have to do is become a positive thinker and my relationship will be better" is not going to cut it. I wish I could tell you that the solution to zapping those toxic thoughts is to *just* think positively. Positive thoughts are helpful to have as you go through life. But, as you will see, it is not enough just to have a positive outlook.

IT TAKES MORE POWER THAN POSITIVE THINKING

I REMEMBER WHEN Jenny, who thought of herself as a "positive person," came to see me after she and her husband Peter had come back from a weekend away. Jenny told me how she walked along the beach, summoning up all her energy and vowing to try to *just* be more positive about her marriage to Peter and appreciate what a nice guy he is. Yet she still found herself wanting to withdraw from Peter and getting angry with him even after she told herself, *I'm going to look at things with Peter more positively.*

As Jenny found, even people with a positive outlook have relationships that become very empty or even fall apart. I have had many positive thinkers end up in my office, absolutely clueless about why they just can't seem to feel satisfied and fulfilled in their relationships. Why? Because when it comes to intimate relationships, no one is immune to toxic thoughts. Toxic thoughts are very sneaky and insidious. Most of us fail to realize how often and intensely toxic thoughts occur outside of our awareness. But don't worry, I'm going to show you surprisingly easy ways to become aware, to finally get the clues you need to control your toxic thinking instead of letting those toxic thoughts control you. I'm also going to show you how, armed with this special form of awareness (which I call relationship mindfulness), you can learn easy-to-apply, yet highly powerful strategies to dispute toxic thoughts. As you learn more about toxic thoughts it will become clear why simply telling yourself, *Okay, I'll just keep thinking positive about my relationship and it will get better* just doesn't work. Trust me, if you do this you'll fall flat on your face. In fact, I bet you've already tried it.

But stay with me; I'm about to give you the tools to help you move light-years ahead on your relationship satisfaction meter. Yes, it will take some work on your behalf. And yes, maintaining a satisfying relationship over time also takes work. Lots of good things in life take work. But I'm going to show you how to take your relationship to the highest level by working at it in a "relationship-smart" way.

Jenny was thrilled to hear that she wasn't going to find the answers to her problems by working *hard* at her relationship. She had to learn to work *smart*. Walking the beach and trying to convince herself that things would get better with Peter only left her feeling more frustrated. But after I worked with Jenny and Peter, she learned some very powerful tools that she could really use to feel better and more satisfied with Peter and their relationship. I'm going to share those tools, and others, with you. Sadly, many people tend to think that relationships are maintenance-free, or that their partners should do the work required to make them happy. That's a nice fantasy, but it's far from the truth.

Once you learn how to appreciate the amazing power of relationship mindfulness, I'm going to teach you a crucial lesson—how to *really* understand what your toxic thoughts are. You can't put out smoldering flames ready to ignite into a raging fire unless you know where the flames originated and in what direction they will spread. I'm going to show you how to extinguish the flames of toxic thinking once and for all. I'm going to show you a very effective but surprisingly simple way to use positive thinking strategies in a new way. You will learn how to address your toxic thoughts every time they arise—and you won't believe how quickly your relationship will improve. It really is amazing.

THE SELF-TALK CONTINUUM			
Triggering Event	*Positive Self-Talk* (Healthy, Realistic)	*Negative Self-Talk* (Occasional, Realistic)	*Toxic Self-Talk* (Frequent, Black-and-White, Unrealistic)
You made an error when balancing checkbook.	"Anyone can mess up once in a while."	"I shouldn't have rushed."	"I've always been a careless person."
You tripped while walking down the street.	"It could have been worse than a bruise."	"I can be really clumsy."	"I can't even take care of myself."
Your boss gave you negative feedback.	"This is a chance to try to learn from my mistakes and improve."	"I should have been better prepared. I screwed up."	"I'll never measure up. I deserve to be fired."

When you begin to explain the events of your life in the all-encompassing, black-and-white style of toxic thoughts, you may have unconsciously programmed your internal tapes with upsetting, unpleasant, extreme thoughts about yourself and others. Such toxic messages may include thoughts like *I can't do anything right, No one wants to marry a bald guy,* or *People who try to be nice like me always get burned in relationships.*

Negative self-talk that becomes extreme, excessive, and distorted will make you feel bad about yourself, others (including your partner), and sometimes even the whole world. That's when self-talk has turned toxic, when you can easily fall into the trap of a negative belief system.

WHY TOXIC THINKING IS SO HARD TO CATCH

ONE OF MY clients, a woman named Tina, came to me because she was unhappy, possibly even depressed. Tina was not successful at dating—she just couldn't meet anyone. She was stuck in a job she hated, still living with her parents at the age of thirty-six, and overweight. "I'm basically a basket case," Tina declared at our first meeting.

When I defined toxic thinking and explained how it might be hampering her ability to change her life, she quickly said, "Oh no! I don't do that. My problem is that I'm depressed."

I provided Tina with written examples of negative self-talk, such as those in the box below.

■

EXAMPLES OF TOXIC SELF-TALK

▶ "If I fail, then I'm a worthless, no-good loser."
▶ "I should be a complete success in everything I do."
▶ "No one will love me because of my problems in life."
▶ "In order to be a worthwhile human being, I need everyone's approval."
▶ "I can't bear disapproval from those who really care about me."
▶ "If I let my guard down and am vulnerable to another person, I will always get burned."
▶ "I can't do anything right."
▶ "I screw up everything in my life."
▶ "People just pretend they like me."
▶ "If people knew about my past failures, they would not respect me at all."

■

I asked Tina to pay attention to her self-talk for one week and to write down what she was thinking. She came to our next session with a notebook. In it was written her random thoughts, such as "You'll be in this job for the rest of your life because you didn't finish college," "Mother can't manage without you so you're stuck here," and "You can't get a date because you're fat. You have no self-control."

Tina was certainly surprised at her own thoughts. She had no idea that she was such a toxic thinker. "It became such a habit, such a routine way of thinking about myself and my life," said Tina, "I didn't even know I was doing it!"

WHY TOXIC SELF-TALKERS DON'T HAVE GOOD RELATIONSHIPS

SOMEONE LIKE TINA, who was making herself miserable in large part because of her toxic thinking, would understandably have difficulty forming a healthy, intimate relationship. She had toxic thoughts that sabotaged her self-esteem and assertiveness. People simply aren't as attracted to negative individuals. Although she said she wanted to be in a relationship, Tina's self-esteem was so poor that she was really terrified of getting involved with someone.

The reality is that most toxic self-talkers do manage to find themselves in intimate relationships—but not healthy ones. Why? Because individuals who are prone to toxic thinking have a hard time relating clearly, reasonably, and openly to an intimate partner. You can't relate well to others if you can't relate well to yourself. The saying "You have to love yourself before you can love anyone else" may sound corny, but it's absolutely true. As you soon will see, in so many cases our toxic thoughts about our partners are not even really *about* our partners—they are about our own issues. Our childhood experiences, commonly referred to as "baggage," often cause us to have unrealistic expectations or "hot buttons" that fuel our toxic thoughts toward our partners.

Was toxic thinking Tina's only problem? No, certainly not. But it was a big part of her problem. Getting rid of the toxic thoughts has helped her change her life in many positive ways. It wasn't always easy and it did take her some time, but Tina is now in a happy relationship. She became aware of how her thoughts caused her problems and she made powerful changes in her thought patterns to solve these problems.

BUT I'M NOT A TOXIC SELF-TALKER!

YOU MAY BE thinking, *Well, this book isn't for me because I'm not a toxic self-talker, so that can't be why I'm frustrated in my relationship. That can't be why I'm not happy with my partner.*

You may even be gleefully thinking, *I knew it. Our relationship problems are not my fault!*

When a couple tells me, "No, no. Toxic thinking isn't *our* problem," but they have a list of things that *are* their problems and often blame each other for those problems, I tell them that, yes, toxic thinking is most likely a factor. At the very least, toxic thinking is a contributor in some form or another, especially if you're having communication problems or difficulty resolving conflicts—two red flags that signify that toxic thinking is at work in your relationship.

Your self-talk may be positive or only occasionally negative when it's about you, but you can still be a toxic thinker when it comes to your partner. You may very well have what I call "partner-directed toxic talk" in your intimate relationship. I believe, based on years of experience, that the vast majority of us are prone to toxic thinking about our intimate partners even if we're not prone to toxic thinking about ourselves.

So before you pronounce yourself and your relationship free of toxic thoughts, I ask you to complete the exercise below, writing down any negative thoughts you may have about yourself and your partner. When I send my clients home with the same exercise, most of them discover that they are indeed prone to toxic thinking in their relationships. Clients who tend to have healthy self-talk when it comes to their perception of themselves often report the opposite when it comes to their relationships. So even if you are a healthy self-talker about yourself, your work, your future, and your friendships, when it comes to your intimate relationship, when it comes to the person you spend the most time with, the person you love the most in the world, you're not out of the woods with toxic thinking yet.

NOT SURE IF YOU'RE A TOXIC THINKER?
TAKE THE SELF-TALK CHALLENGE AND FIND OUT!

YOU MAY NOT think you're a toxic self-talker. You may be a positive self-talker who has very healthy self-esteem. I hope so. But it's possible that you are a toxic self-talker and *you just don't know it.* Before you assume that you don't have this problem, please complete this test to discover what you're thinking about yourself and your partner. You may be in for a big surprise.

This exercise is simple. For a few days, remind yourself to listen to your self-talk. Every time you catch yourself thinking something about yourself or your partner, write it down on a piece of paper under the following headings:

THOUGHTS YOU HAVE ABOUT YOURSELF		
Positive (Healthy, Realistic Despite Problems/Obstacles) Example: *I'm doing well today in spite of my boss' bad mood.*	*Negative* (Occasional Gray Area) Example: *Lately, everything seems to be going against me.*	*Toxic* (Frequent Black-and-White Thoughts) Example: *I can never do anything right.*

THOUGHTS YOU HAVE ABOUT YOUR PARTNER		
Positive (Healthy, Realistic Despite Problems/Obstacles) Example: *We need to work on this issue.*	**Negative** (Occasional Gray Area) Example: *I wish she wouldn't do that anymore. It drives me crazy.*	**Toxic** (Frequent Black-and-White Thoughts) Example: *There she goes again. She's going to put us in the poorhouse.*

As you complete this exercise, remember that the difference between negative thinking and toxic thinking is frequency and degree. If you eat a hot fudge sundae during your favorite television show and then feel bad about yourself for hours or days afterward *I'm a no good fatso,* that's toxic thinking. If your boyfriend forgot your big weekend plans, you may think, *He's so distracted and scattered today,* which is negative, but the thought *I can't handle his ADHD* is toxic, because you're describing your partner in a negative and most likely inaccurate way. You're not describing a situation or experience, but your interpretation of your partner's actions. If your husband is late and you're telling yourself, *Maybe his car broke down,* that's a reasonable way to explain his lateness. If you jump to the conclusion *He's dead* or *He's cheating on me,* that's an extreme, black-and-white toxic thought.

TOXIC THINKING HAS A POWERFUL INFLUENCE OVER HOW WE FEEL

TOXIC THINKING HAS such a powerful effect because *your toxic thoughts profoundly influence how you feel.* This is one of the most important points to understand about toxic thinking. The thoughts we have when we talk to ourselves don't just go in and out of our heads. They stick. Our feelings, moods, and actions are driven by our self-talk. I'm sure you have heard yourself or someone you know say, "I don't know why, but I feel so close to him today," or "I can't figure out why I'm so angry with her." There's no mystery. This is proof of the power of your underlying self-talk. Your thoughts can either make you feel good about your partner and your relationship (if they are positive thoughts) or disappointed, angry, or sad about your partner and your relationship (if they are toxic thoughts).

If you're telling yourself over and over again that your boyfriend is irresponsible and lazy, what feelings are you going to have about him? Bad ones! You're going to feel like you're involved with an irresponsible, lazy guy. How could you not feel that way?

If your internal self-talk tape constantly plays the thought *She's holding me back,* you will end up focusing on all of those experiences that prove to you that your partner is holding you back. You are going to feel bad about yourself for letting her hold you back. You are going to feel bad about her; after all, she's the one preventing you from realizing your dreams. And you're going to feel badly about your life in general—how could you not when your dreams have been thwarted in this way? You are going to create your own reality; that you are being robbed of something because *she is holding you back.*

What kind of relationship can you have with these types of thoughts swirling around in your head? Not a very strong one.

You can also make yourself physically sick. If you're a toxic self-talker, you might have high blood pressure or a nervous stomach. Maybe you suffer from headaches or gain weight. When we talk toxic, we feel toxic—stressed, tired, and oftentimes depressed and anxious.

So, even if you don't realize that you're telling yourself something toxic about your partner (because we often self-talk without realizing it), toxic talk still silently and strongly influences the way you feel and behave. If you constantly repeat a toxic thought about your partner day after day or during argument after argument *He can't do anything right* or *She's an impossible nag,* eventually you will perceive that toxic statement as reality—even if it's not reality.

TOXIC THINKING CREATES ITS OWN REALITY

THINK ABOUT THAT fact for a moment—*even if it's not reality.* That's a powerful statement. It's also scary, isn't it? We can turn our thoughts into reality—thoughts that we may not even be aware we're having! This means that even if we're not unattractive to the opposite sex, we can actually convince ourselves, and therefore others, that we *are* just by thinking such a thing about ourselves. That is scary!

In my field, you'll often hear the phrase "What you resist will persist." So true! Toxic thoughts will not just go away by themselves. After thousands of hours practicing psychotherapy with people from all walks of life, I can tell you that many people think that they can ignore or outrun their toxic thoughts—they're wrong. Over and over I have seen couples at various breaking points, with one or both partners feeling anxious or depressed, and turning to food, alcohol, or drugs for comfort. Most of the time toxic thinking is an important contributor, if not the main contributor, to these problems. Often these couples have come to therapy only after their toxic thoughts have been affecting their perception for years. They're so exhausted from trying to outrun and ignore their toxic thoughts that they feel desperate and are willing to seek professional help.

CONTROL YOUR TOXIC THOUGHTS BEFORE THEY CONTROL YOU

FROM OUR EARLIEST ancestors, we have been influenced—for better or worse—by the way we look at situations and talk to ourselves about those situations. The Roman philosopher, Epictetus, explained this fact thousands of years ago. He said, "Man is not disturbed by events alone, but by his *perception* of events."

Following Epictetus, doesn't it stand to reason that we can actually change our perception of events by detoxifying our thinking? Imagine the freedom we could enjoy if we stopped beating up on ourselves and our intimate partners. Think how much better we'd all feel if we could deal with the real issues of our relationships instead of the toxic ones that lead us off on tangents.

The truth is that you can actually feel better by modifying how you think about yourself. So, instead of thinking the toxic thought that you are being irresponsible, think the more positive thought that you made an honest mistake, or you had a key learning experience. Instead of being lazy, you had a recharging period. Instead of being a failure, you had a setback or you are closer to a solution.

Do you think you would start feeling differently about yourself if you could detoxify your toxic thoughts?

You'd better believe it!

And do you think you would start to feel better about your partner if you could detoxify your thinking about him or her?

You'd better believe that, too!

The ability to rethink and work through your toxic thoughts is the key to feeling good about yourself *and* others. It's also the key to taking positive action. By applying the new set of more healthy, realistic, and positive thinking skills you will learn in the chapters ahead, you will be able to rid your life of the toxic thoughts that are undermining your happiness.

BUT WHAT IF I CAN'T GET RID OF MY TOXIC THINKING?

YOU *CAN* LEARN to rethink the frustrating and stressful situations in your life—especially in your intimate relationships. So if you're surprised or disappointed to discover that you're a toxic thinker, don't panic. I've worked with individuals and couples with pretty serious cases of toxic thinking and they've all been able to break the habit because they wanted to change and remained committed to the healthy, positive changes they made.

The tools in this book will help you behave and even feel differently about yourself, your situation, and the people in your life. Imagine the possibilities! By thinking differently, instead of being "so angry I could just kill my husband," you can be "peeved at him." Instead of thinking that your girlfriend "overwhelms me," she can "be demanding sometimes." Instead of being "rejected," you will be "misunderstood." Instead of being "unable to communicate," you will be "experiencing some difficulty understanding each other." I'm not just talking about changing words; I'm talking about changing perceptions and feelings. It's pretty powerful stuff!

There is no question about it: *The way we think about events in our lives directly influences how we feel about those events and ourselves—for better or worse.*

The good news is that we can control our behavior by controlling our feelings. The exciting news is that when you apply this new set of thinking skills to your relationship, you'll be surprised at how you and your intimate partner will feel closer and more fulfilled than you ever would have imagined.

TO SUM IT ALL UP

WE ARE ALL prone to dissatisfaction in our intimate relationships—human beings are just built that way. But trust me, the fact that your partner can't read your mind, that she isn't your soul mate, or any other reason you have given yourself for your unhappiness is not the real cause. It all comes back to the toxic thinking in your head.

Over time, partners will often experience negative feelings toward each other (like mild frustration, disappointment, or dissatisfaction) over such things as less attention, affection, time together, or sex than desired. When couples start out in their relationships, the infatuation they experience suspends the reality of the daily stresses that wear on longer relationships. No relationship can fulfill idealized, unrealistic, and overly positive expectations. We need look no further than differences about money, parenting, or handling the in-laws to see that many aspects of relationships are not pleasant.

Negative thoughts about your partner in response to such issues is one thing, but toxic thinking about your partner is another. Toxic thoughts are irrational and cause you to feel excessive levels of anger, resentment, disappointment, frustration, anxiety, or depression. When you are blinded by these toxic thoughts and full of toxic feelings, you are in no shape to work on your relationship. No relationship can be perfect, yet many people feel they should be. Unless you marry a true god or goddess whose sole purpose is to please you (and this person does not exist), you will need to continue to find constructive ways to deal with the inevitable miscommunications, misinterpretations, misunderstandings, and all the other "mis-es" that are the reality of relationships and the triggers of toxic thinking.

You need to lose your fantasies of having a partner who can read your mind, solve all your problems, or know exactly what to say. Instead, let me show you how *your* understanding of how your own mind works when it comes to your intimate relationship is the surest way to get more out of your relationship—more than you ever could have imagined.

2 Toxic Thoughts: The Silent Relationship Killer

HERE'S THE REAL bottom line on relationship communication that no one has ever told you: *Before you can begin to communicate with your partner about problems and issues, you must first be able to think clearly and rationally about your partner and your problems and issues.*

Toxic thinking makes clear thinking very difficult. Before you can tell your partner how you really feel about him or her, how a problem or issue makes you feel, and what you need to make it better, you have to first be able to state the problem or issue. In order to do that, you must be able to think clearly and rationally about what's happening in your relationship.

Most people facing relationship problems simply fail to see how their thoughts, healthy or toxic, can affect their relationship. They fail to recognize toxic thinking at work because they don't know how to look for it. No one teaches us about the devastating effects of toxic thinking on communication before we go out on a date, move in together, or get married. But once you understand how toxic thinking works, you will probably find that it is undermining some aspect of your relationship or other areas of your life.

OUR CULTURE ENCOURAGES TOXIC THINKING ABOUT RELATIONSHIPS

TO A LARGE extent, our society reinforces the negative habit of thinking toxically about our partners. We see sitcoms on television where partners of one gender bash the other. We see couples in crisis on many afternoon talk shows. There are magazines that are dedicated to repairing and saving relationships. We see a fifty percent divorce rate and begin to internalize the toxic thought that relationship dissatisfaction is our destiny. Relationships are strained and damaged over time by toxic thinking habits, and partners convince themselves that they are no longer "in love."

All too often, toxic thoughts about an intimate partner become ingrained habits that you may only recognize as a general sense of anger or frustration. *If you can't think about your conflicts in a healthy, helpful way, then you can't begin to talk about them or solve them.*

TOXIC THINKING SHORT-CIRCUITS GENUINE COMMUNICATION

THOUGH THERE ARE a variety of reasons why we think toxically in relationships, the end result is always the same—communication suffers badly.

Like an onion with many hidden layers, there are underlying (often toxic) thoughts behind what we say out loud and what we feel. Sadly, these toxic thoughts can cause us far more tears than any onion!

The first and most critical problem couples often have isn't with their communication, it's their tendency to think on a toxic level. Toxic thinking by one or both partners often prevents or short-circuits genuine communication between them.

THE THREE-D EFFECT CAUSED BY TOXIC THINKING

COUPLES WITH TOXIC thinking problems often exhibit what I call The Three-D Effect in their communication: Distraction, Distance, and Disconnect.

Distraction

Have you ever been engaged in an argument but couldn't remember how or why it started?

If you answered yes, this is toxic thinking at work.

Toxic thinking distracts couples from focusing on their real problems and understanding the real issues in the relationship. Toxic thinking erodes communication because it keeps you from resolving what truly needs to be resolved. When couples can't resolve their true issues, it leads to even more anger and hurt feelings.

This was the case for Dan and Robin, an exasperated couple who came to see me because they had found that their toxic thoughts distracted them from effective communication. "It's like we can't talk without bringing up all these other problems and things we don't like about each other. We're just stuck in this crazy pattern," Robin said. If and when Dan and Robin attempted to discuss their problems, they became sidetracked by the fact that Robin had called Dan *selfish* and Dan had said that Robin's moodiness *always* wrecked their good times. Fortunately, I was able to help Dan and Robin get past this early, distraction stage of The Three-D Effect. As you'll see in more detail later, Dan and Robin's types of toxic statements—Label Slinging, and The All or Nothing Trap—created a huge distraction from the real issue. If this couple stayed stuck on Dan being selfish, or Robin always being moody, they would not have been able to work together in a mature, give-and-take way to address the actual issue at hand—in their case, Robin's desire to go back to school. Most couples are simply unable to address their real problems because toxic thinking sidetracks them so much that they can't "see" the real problem or issue.

Toxic thinking usually sends one or both partners on a mission to prove their innocence of the charges being leveled at them. For Robin and Dan, it went something like this:

Dan: "I'm not selfish. Just last week I watched the baby three days in a row and made dinner every night so you could have a break . . ."

Robin: "I don't always wreck our good time. Didn't we have fun at the Martins's dinner party . . . ?"

Round and round it goes. Arguing this way is exhausting! If this couple can even remember why they're arguing in the first place, they will probably be too tired and fed up to even talk about it.

The distraction created by toxic thinking inevitably causes partners to become frustrated with one another. It is one of the worst side effects of toxic thinking. This is the point at which I hear couples say things like "He doesn't understand me," "She's so unreasonable!," or "I can never get through to him."

Distance

When partners become frustrated, they become distant from one another. When the distance starts settling in, partners usually either lash out with more toxic talk or shut down into a toxic silence. The fact is that nothing can threaten the balance of your thinking more than the fear of loss from your partner. By this I mean the fear of loss of respect, love, or commitment. Partners plagued by toxic thoughts toward one another end up saying terrible things because they are in a highly aroused emotional state. The partners are in this emotionally destructive state because they fear being threatened or hurt. In the grip of toxic thoughts, which inevitably trigger hypersensitivity and misinterpretations of the other's intentions, the partners usually lash out to defend themselves. However, each partner lashes out with toxic statements or actions that can do great damage to the other partner.

You know how frustrated your partner can make you feel. We've all been there. In a desperate attempt to "reach" the person, we sometimes get caught up in our own frustration and then go overboard. We can sometimes say terrible and hurtful things. I hear people say, "I just lost it," or "I don't know what came over me. I couldn't help myself."

What came over you was your toxic thinking! Toxic thinking causes you to spin out of control. Robin may genuinely start out just wanting to "get through" to Dan or "be heard" by him, but what she ends up doing is verbalizing all the toxic thoughts she had had about him, like "I don't know why I ever married you," "I'm starting to think I made a huge mistake," or "You're just like your father."

Dan, on the other hand, may not lash out when he becomes frustrated—many people, both men and women, don't lash out. Instead, they shut down. If you've ever been on the receiving end of a "silent treatment," or have dealt with a partner who won't even talk about the issues, then you know how much more frustrated you may feel in dealing with this person. But you should realize that it is equally aggravating for them. Imagine the level of frustration that Dan is feeling if he can't even try to work it out with Robin? Instead, he's thinking his own toxic thoughts, such as *Nothing I say can make a difference with her. She's totally unreasonable.*

Disconnect

If enough distraction occurs to feed the distance between Robin and Dan, one or both partners may shut down as a result of each partner's inability to "reach" or "get through" to the other. This is when couples disconnect. One or both partners have lost the ability to empathize with the other. As you'll come to understand throughout this book, empathy is the glue that holds relationships together.

Though I see couples at every "D," most couples come to see me at this disconnection stage. This is the most terrifying of the Three Ds—when you have lost the ability to see or appreciate your partner's point of view and he or she has lost the ability to see yours. This is the point at which people report feeling intense loneliness in their relationship. It's very sad and painful to watch.

Dan may say, "I feel like we're just going through the motions." Robin may say, "I don't feel like I know him anymore." One of the partners typically becomes fed up with the emotional emptiness and threatens to leave. At this point each partner is literally not sure how to think, act, and feel with the other. It is both tragic and fascinating to see how partners who often have been together for many years and who knew each others' most intimate eating, bathroom, and sexual habits become total strangers to one another.

Instead of repairing the damage, they spiral into toxic thought patterns and may fatalistically begin to think such destructive thoughts as *What am I doing even trying with her, this is not the person who I first met and/or married!*

Many couples disconnect and start giving up on the relationship. Separation, breakup, and divorce are very likely.

IS YOUR RELATIONSHIP AT RISK?

OKAY, SO HOW do you know to what extent *your* relationship is suffering from toxic thinking? You may already see aspects of yourself or your relationship in Dan and Robin's situation—many people do.

For most couples, however, toxic-thinking problems are revealed most clearly in two ways: your "argument style" and your true feelings about the relationship.

Your argument style is how you fight with your partner, what you say and how you say it when your emotions are running high. Though you may have toxic thoughts about your partner that you don't verbalize, toxic thoughts usually turn into toxic statements that start flying during the heat of an argument. It's hard not to try to punish or wound your partner when you're feeling emotional, betrayed, upset, or misunderstood. And your tendency to hurl toxic statements at your partner dramatically increases when they're being hurled at you.

THE WARNING SIGNS OF TOXIC FIGHTING

YOUR RELATIONSHIP MAY be suffering the negative effects of toxic thinking if one or more of the following statements is true. In at least two out of three of your most recent arguments, you and your partner:

1. often end up arguing about something other than the original problem or issue.
2. can't remember why your argument started.
3. label the other partner negatively (such as "couch potato," "lazy," "selfish," or "nag").
4. feel like you can't make the other partner understand how you feel.
5. say things you later regret.
6. apologize for saying something mean to your partner even though you still believe it's true.
7. use words like "always," "never," and "should" when referring to your partner.
8. bring up past issues or arguments—even ones that you thought were resolved—in a hostile way during current arguments.
9. have declared certain topics "off-limits" during arguments, but have a hard time staying away from them.
10. exaggerate or accuse the other partner of exaggerating the situation or problem.
11. end up using bad argument behavior, such as screaming, blaming, name-calling, door slamming, kicking one partner out of the house, or locking doors.
12. feel like the other partner "pushes your buttons" or says mean things on purpose to get a reaction out of you.
13. are unable to simply discuss problems—it always turns into an argument.

EXAMINE YOUR TRUE FEELINGS

NOW, LET'S LOOK at the other way that most couples can assess the extent to which toxic thinking is threatening their relationship—through their feelings. One of the keys to detoxifying your thinking about your partner is to become aware of your feelings about him or her.

Remember, thoughts create reality. That reality in turn creates feelings. Strong, negative feelings often arise from toxic thinking. So it makes perfect sense that one of the best ways to detect your toxic thinking is to tune in to your feelings. While not exhaustive, the list below includes the most common feelings that underlie toxic thinking in intimate relationships.

FEELINGS THAT SIGNAL TOXIC THINKING IN RELATIONSHIPS		
Angry	Cheated	Unappreciated
Sad	Disgusted	Neglected
Upset	Disappointed	Self-Conscious
Afraid	Hurt	Misunderstood
Threatened	Frustrated	Pressured
Shamed	Humiliated	Enraged
Unloved	Rejected	Discouraged

It is very important that both partners realize that any of the above feelings can signal toxic thinking. In particular, feeling unloved, rejected, hurt, or neglected typically leads people to make critical or nagging comments. How sadly ironic! What we really want is more love, acceptance, and attention, but when those needs are frustrated, we respond with toxic thoughts. Those toxic thoughts, in turn, create negative feelings and result in critical, hurtful comments and outrage about all kinds of petty annoyances.

How sad that love turns so quickly to resentment.

But if partners can see the underlying reasons for the hurt and anger, the entire interaction can change. The hurtful comments are disarmed. The criticism is seen as merely a way for your lover, who wants to be more loving with you, to vent his or her temporary frustration. You can then see the hurt and wounded person behind the attacking appearance. If a couple can become understanding, get closer, and show they care, the relationship can be turned around. This is where the power of empathy can be extremely helpful. In Chapter Eight I will explain more about empathy and how to master this relationship enhancing skill.

How powerful are our feelings? Very! They influence our actions not only in our intimate relationships, but in all other aspects of our lives. People purchase items they cannot afford because of feelings.

Many have made life-changing decisions because of what *feels right.* Multimillion-dollar business deals break down because of feelings. Terrifying incidents of road rage occur because of feelings. While the answer to this question may seem painfully obvious, we often forget a very important truth: *By controlling our toxic thinking, we can control our feelings.*

The tools in this book will help you to be more aware of your toxic thoughts. Awareness of your thoughts and feelings requires discipline and commitment. To have a healthy body you must feed it the right nutrients and minimize the intake of unhealthy foods. In the same vein, you must feed your mind with healthy, nontoxic thoughts to ensure that your feelings remain positive and strong about yourself and your relationship.

Toxic thoughts create a spiral that fuels toxic feelings, and the consequences are negative statements and actions. For example, Joanne toxically thinks that her husband Bob is "never putting our family first" after he calls to inform her that he will be home late from work because of a last-minute crisis. This toxic thought propels her to feel hurt, which leads her to say to Bob, "Fine, but don't expect dinner to be ready and all of us to be smiling cheerfully when you walk in."

Bob, on the other hand, is tired and has had a miserable day at work. The last thing he wants is to stay late at work, but his boss is riding him again, so what can he do? It's not like he can just quit his job. He responds to Joanne, "Well, maybe I won't bother coming home!"

Over time, these types of toxic thoughts, feelings, and statements lead both people to feel an increasing sense of dissatisfaction with the relationship.

■

HOW DO YOU REALLY FEEL ABOUT YOUR RELATIONSHIP?

HERE ARE NINE warning signs that your relationship may be in trouble because of toxic thinking. You:

1. find yourself frequently irritated with your partner, whether or not he or she is actually near you.

2. no longer do nice things for each other, such as saying "thank you," complimenting each other, sending an occasional love note, giving little presents, or sending flowers.

3. talk to someone else more than you do to your partner, especially if the conversations are about being unhappy with your spouse and/or how attractive someone else is.

4. seldom remember good times together or share your hopes and ideas.

5. don't try to do fun things with your partner.

6. are bored or disinterested with sex, and avoid your partner by sleeping, working, drinking, playing sports, doing community work, etc.

7. feel hopeless about being able to improve your relationship.

8. believe you are criticized or judged by your partner, even when you are not engaged in an argument.

9. wonder what's wrong with your partner. Why can't she (he) read your mind? Why doesn't she (he) just know what you need? After all, aren't soul mates supposed to be able to do these things?

■

MAKE THE COMMITMENT TO THINK YOUR WAY BACK TO LOVE

THERE ARE MANY powerful tools in this book to help you free your relationship from toxic thinking. But all the tools in the world will not help you unless you know that you need them. Self-awareness and relationship awareness are critical in the journey back to love. Being self-aware means you choose to recognize where you are making mistakes. You examine how you feel and how those feelings can be fueled by toxic thoughts. You make an effort to figure out what aspects of your thinking, actions, and reactions aren't helping you have a happy relationship. And once you know what is causing your problems, you decide to take the necessary steps to resolve them.

Relationship awareness is critical too. Make a promise to yourself right now. Say, "I will be aware that my relationship requires work because all relationships are prone to misconceptions, misperceptions, misunderstandings, and lots of other 'mis-es'!"

If you were handed a great work of art, you would handle it with care. Is this not how you first felt about your partner? Why not honor your partner in the same way? Thinking your way back to love starts with being aware of how precious your relationship is.

Awareness—both of yourself and your relationship—is your first step to restoring or repairing genuine, healthy communication in your relationship. The second step is to figure out which of the nine toxic thought patterns may be undermining your communication.

In the next chapter, you will learn about the nine types of toxic thoughts that are hazards to intimacy. I think of these nine destructive toxic thought patterns as *toxidants*. Please read with an open mind. Be willing to see yourself in the many examples of how toxic thinking undermines healthy communication.

As you will discover, healthy and positive thoughts toward your intimate partner are what I call the *anti-toxidants*. I will show you step-by-step how to apply these anti-toxidants to improve or save your relationship. Anti-toxidants will help you think your way back to love and a better relationship. I'll even hand you a map that clearly shows you how to get back to that place of joy and discovery in your relationship.

Actually, what I will give you is a MAP. This is my easy but powerful three-step model for thinking your way back to love. But first, it's time you were introduced to the specific toxic thought patterns that may be ruining your relationship.

3 The Nine Toxic Thought Patterns That Ruin Relationships

NOW YOU KNOW the truth—we all have toxic thoughts that wreak havoc on our intimate relationships. You may even feel lucky that your partner can't really read your mind and find out that you have toxic thoughts. But trust me, these toxic thoughts don't just go away. They lead us to think our way out of love.

But what exactly are the specific types of toxic thoughts? That is what I'm going to share with you now. Once you understand these toxic thought patterns, you will see just how much your relationship success begins and ends with you and what is going on in your head.

I was inspired by my own experience with couples and the ideas of David Burns, M.D., Aaron Beck, M.D., and Albert Ellis, Ph.D., as I formed the framework for my theory of these nine toxic thought patterns. What I've done is taken the sound, heavily researched principles and strategies of cognitive therapy and presented them to you in the context of intimate relationships—in an easy-to-understand and easy-to-apply format.

Learning about these nine toxic thought patterns will take some work. But compared to dealing with the devastating consequences of most broken intimate relationships and marriages, this is a breeze. Trust me, it's worth the work.

BEGIN WITH GOOD INTENTIONS

YOU MAY DISCOVER one, two, or even all nine of these toxic thought patterns at work in your relationship. You may be a number four toxic thinker while your husband or wife is a number five or a number eight toxic thinker. The goal of familiarizing yourself with these toxic thought patterns is not so you can label yourself or your partner. This is not about getting ammunition to use against your partner so you can win an argument or make a point. The point is to help you get to know yourself and your thoughts better, so you can discover how those thoughts make you feel about your partner and your relationship. By understanding your toxic thoughts, you can soon become a better and happier person in your relationship—more able to think clearly, to understand your motivations, and to resolve your conflicts.

Try to read the descriptions of the nine toxic thought patterns with an open and quiet mind. You don't want to read through this section while you're angry or upset with your partner—you'll wind up looking for evidence rather than illumination. Though you may instantly discover yourself or your partner in one or more of these toxic thought patterns, it's just as common not to "see it" until you're having an issue with your partner or you're in the middle of an argument. Then, it happens. Ding! You suddenly find yourself thinking, *Okay, this seems familiar.* This happens a lot, too.

Keep in mind that each of us varies in our toxic thinking threshold. Some partners may fall more readily into toxic thinking than others. The bottom line is that most of us do fall into toxic thinking at times, and if it's ignored, it can be very damaging.

Here they are, the nine toxic thought patterns that ruin relationships:

#1: The All or Nothing Trap

Jack is considerate to his wife Sophie in many ways. He does the laundry because he knows that with three kids it's hard for her to keep up with it. He fills her car with gas. He tiptoes around in the morning so she can get a little extra sleep. But he does have the habit of leaving dirty dishes in the sink. Unfortunately, finding dirty dishes in the sink is the one thing that drives Sophie crazy, even crazier than when he folds the laundry and just leaves it sitting there on top of the dryer. Why can't he just rinse the dishes and put them in the dishwasher? Doesn't he realize he's just making more work for her? It's like he doesn't respect her time or the fact that she is not only working full time, but also does most of the housework. She's asked him time and time again to please rinse his dishes and put them in the dishwasher. Worn down with toxic thoughts, Sophie doesn't consider how Jack helps with the laundry or fills the car with gas. Those aren't the things she really cares about. All she can think as she's putting his dishes away is that he never thinks about her feelings. Why, she wants to know, is he always so inconsiderate? Jack, on the other hand, wants to know why nothing he does is ever good enough for her.

Welcome to the all-too-common and destructive world of All or Nothing toxic thinking. There's a reason why I discuss The All or Nothing Trap first. Based on many hours of listening to distressed and exasperated couples, this toxic thought problem is, without a doubt, the most common of them all. If I had a dollar for every "always" and "never" I've heard from couples in distress, I'd be on a tropical island instead of in my office.

When you're upset with your partner, and feel misunderstood or hurt, it's very easy to lapse into the black-and-white mindset that characterizes All or Nothing thinking. By black-and-white mindset I mean the tendency by one or both partners to see the other as either completely positive or completely negative. He's *never* competent. She's *always* saying the worst thing. My husband gets it wrong *every* time.

There is no "in between" when partners see each other in an All or Nothing way. You may very well feel that your partner never listens to you or is always inconsiderate. However, this is not likely the reality. Most people have a range of behavior that includes being considerate and being inconsiderate. This range of behavior is shaped from a combination of our genes and our upbringing. As individuals we vary in both pleasant behaviors (like giving compliments) and unpleasant ones (like interrupting). While I am a believer in the fundamental goodness of human beings, there are some people who do bring extremely undesirable behaviors to relationships, such as active addictions, venomous manipulations, and abuse. In most cases, however, it is the work of our All or Nothing toxic thoughts that lead us to unfavorably exaggerate our partner's undesirable behaviors.

So why do we do this? We fall into All or Nothing thinking toward our partners to alleviate the stress and tension it causes us when their statements or actions don't make sense to us (*How could he not know that always leaving dishes in the sink drives me nuts?*) or don't fulfill our needs (*She never supports me*). The extremes of All or Nothing thinking reduce emotional tension by giving us a convenient, easy-to-understand way to explain our partners' bothersome behaviors.

Take, for example, Kate and her fiancé Adam. Kate is frustrated with Adam because "he never listens." In Kate's idealistic, black-and-white vision of the relationship, Adam is always ready, willing, and able to listen to what she has to say. When your expectations are not met—when Adam falls asleep on the couch when Kate has an important issue to discuss—you will inevitably grow frustrated, bitter, or fed up. This creates tension, and humans seek to reduce tension. So, in the face of these inconsistencies, we attempt to simplify our partners' behaviors in our minds with All or Nothing thinking. This is about self-protection *(It's not my fault. I'm not the one who always falls asleep)*. You need to explain to yourself why your needs aren't being met and why you're not the culprit. Unfortunately, All or Nothing thinking is far more destructive than protective. When you tell your partner, "You always . . . " or "You never . . . " I can guarantee that you and your partner will not be discussing your real issues.

All or Nothing thoughts illustrate how, once verbalized, toxic thoughts distract couples from their real issues. If you're telling your wife, "You never listen . . . " or your boyfriend, "You always ignore me when I'm upset," these kinds of statements will inevitably cause the other person to try and defend him- or herself. The inevitable return volley of "Well, how about what you always do to me . . . " or "I do not always ignore you. Just last night we talked for two hours but you obviously did not hear a single word I said . . . " then ensues instead of productive problem-solving.

Okay, so maybe you are better with finances and your husband is better at setting limits with the kids. That is fine and it may be true. The toxic All or Nothing thinking problems occur, however, when you start to generalize too much. It's when your husband overspends and you say to yourself, *I can't rely on him for anything* instead of reminding yourself that he is only human and does meet your other needs. Or you forget to follow through on a consequence for the kids and your husband thinks, *She has no interest whatsoever in teaching the kids right from wrong,* instead of realizing that you are feeling overwhelmed and discouraged.

What I try to stress to couples is that no one is perfect. You are not perfect, and, of course, your intimate partner is not perfect. As a good friend of mine says, "The only perfect people are in the cemetery!" Intellectually, we know that people have a range of abilities and weaknesses. Being realistic in your relationship means seeing yourself and your partner on a continuum of strengths and weaknesses. Being in a healthy, vital relationship means that you don't see your partner in All or Nothing terms.

#2: Catastrophic Conclusions

Claire is furious with Joel. He is spending more money than they had planned on a part-time business venture in which he recently became involved. She's begun to fantasize about them losing their house and cars. When her fantasies became too vivid and frightening to keep to herself, she snaps at him, saying, "You're ruining us. You're running us into the ground." In response to his wife's outburst, Joel develops catastrophic thoughts of his own: "She just wants us to go on the same way as always, paycheck to paycheck. She has no faith in me. She thinks I'm a loser and that I'm going to fail."

Another common toxic thinking pattern is jumping to Catastrophic Conclusions. One partner exaggerates negative actions and events concerning the other partner. A missed bill is distorted as bankruptcy. A week without sexual contact gets exaggerated into "You don't find me sexy anymore," or "We're going to have a sexless marriage." Conflicted feelings are frequently perceived as hypocrisy, as in the case of a woman I worked with who viewed her husband's ambivalence toward buying a new house as his determination to make her unhappy.

Partners who have unresolved "emotional ghosts" from their pasts are particularly at risk for Catastrophic Conclusions. I can easily argue that we all have some emotional ghosts from our pasts. But the more important point is the extent to which they still haunt you. For many people, childhood was not a bed of roses. If family problems (such as emotional or physical abandonment, addictions, financial stress, mental illness, body-image problems, peer difficulties, learning disabilities, and many other types of issues) are not worked through and understood as children and teens, they can predispose adults to use toxic thought patterns toward their partners.

For example, growing up with a father with a gambling problem, or growing up without a sense of financial stability can easily trigger your fear that your partner is going to ruin your credit or that he's spending too much money. If a mother seemingly favored one sibling over another, this could trigger feelings of abandonment that lead to toxic thoughts and statements such as "You always care more about your mother's feelings than mine."

Even just growing up with a pessimistic or negative parent can influence you to conclude the worst. Please be reassured, however, that even if you grew up with depressed parents, this does not have to be your destiny. No matter what emotional baggage you have from your upbringing, there is always hope. In Chapter Seven, I talk a lot more about emotional ghosts and how to keep them from causing toxic thoughts.

Presented another way, Catastrophic Conclusions are highly negative, exaggerated predictions. These fatalistic, toxic Catastrophic Conclusions block partners from working out problems together. With catastrophic thinking, the toxicity spreads from irrational beliefs about the partner's actions to perceptions of the relationship itself, spurring thoughts like *This whole marriage is now blown to bits.*

One of the ironies of Catastrophic Conclusions is that they can lead not only to a breakdown of trust and communication, but to the very catastrophic event feared by the partner who is having this type of toxic thought. Jerry, for example, felt threatened because his wife Elizabeth was spending more time with her girlfriend who'd just become single after a divorce. The girlfriend's marriage had ended because of the woman's infidelity. Jerry, who was feeling insecure in his relationship, jumped to the Catastrophic Conclusion that *I can never trust Elizabeth as long as she's with that no-good friend of hers. They're going to go out and meet men. This is going to ruin our marriage.* And Jerry's catastrophizing indeed nearly broke the couple apart. Fortunately, Jerry was able to work through his Catastrophic Conclusions before his wife left him.

#3: The *Should* Bomb

Dave knows that his wife Diana's low-paying job in an animal rescue shelter is important to her, but he feels that she should know how much financial pressure he's under. He feels that for the sake of the family, she should want to get a job making more money. Diana feels that Dave should know how personally important her work with animals is. They fight bitterly about what each one thinks the other should do and think.

Despite the silent frustrations and wishful thinking suggested by the title of this book, most of us occasionally need to be reminded that our partners are not mind readers. When the *Should* Bomb hits, one partner assumes the other will meet one or more of his or her needs—because he or she should just *know* that you need a hug or could use a break. We become angry and frustrated and wonder, *Why can't you read my mind?*

Like all intimacy-crushing toxic thoughts, *should*s are not the result of one partner waking up in the morning and saying, "I want to be mean to my partner today." Toxic *should*s can result from a sense of expectation, sometimes rooted in our childhoods and other past relationships. For example, a man whose mother was hard on him (for his own good) as a child may expect that his wife *should* be the same way to their son, or a wife who was told all her life by her parents to figure out problems on her own may feel that her husband *should* know to keep his distance when she's frustrated. We often unknowingly bring these expectations into our relationships.

But just as often, Hollywood fantasies and unrealistic expectations about how a relationship *should* be and how your partner *should* treat you are to blame for triggering the *Should* Bomb toxic thought pattern. "I thought soul mate meant mind reader," said one woman who couldn't seem to find a satisfying relationship. I'm sorry, but it doesn't.

Another client admitted that her excessive *should*s toward her husband were related to her romanticized views of what a stepfamily should be like (for example like the Brady Bunch). She initially felt that her husband *should* want to spend just as much uninterrupted time with her biological children as with his own. As I helped her examine the complexities of their situation, with different custody arrangements and the fragile state of the children after divorce, she adjusted her expectations and interpretations of her husband's desires and actions.

Like all toxic thoughts, *should*s often occur outside of our immediate awareness. Yet they are there—often as a result of unrealistic, demanding needs that we place on our partners. When our partners do not meet these needs, we attribute our anger to negative qualities in our partners. This is a major mistake. Every *should* do can blind you to what your partner *would* or *could* do. Said another way, *should*s lead you to unfairly block out the strengths and good intentions of your partner.

#4: Label Slinging

Jennifer and Scott are thinking about getting married, but they have some issues that need to be worked out before making the final commitment—like the fact that Scott thinks Jennifer is a "shopaholic." Jennifer feels her shopping habits are not extreme, but Scott, who grew up in a frugal household, judges her by an extreme standard. Jennifer resents being labeled, and in turn calls Scott "the world's ultimate couch potato," which she says is not an insult, but just a joke.

Labels are so easy and convenient—what better way to express the frustration, anger, and resentment you have about your partner than to sum them up in a short and sweet statement that gets the message across? Usually the message a label conveys is: "Mr. Couch Potato, I don't like when you sit there and waste the only time we'll have together this weekend."

I often see an unfortunate paradox with toxic labeling. People who assign labels to their partners are often using these labels to avoid how they really feel—angry or frustrated. Yet the label they project onto their partners often reflects areas of dissatisfaction in themselves. I saw this in a husband who labeled his wife as an unorganized slob, yet his own haphazard, inconsistent style had cost him his job. Partners who label are trying to use these labels to avoid dealing with the conflicts at hand. Conflicts not discussed can't be resolved. Unresolved conflicts erode relationships.

Label Slinging is also hazardous to your relationship because labels can injure your perception of your intimate partner and your partner's perception of him- or herself. When Label Slinging occurs, the labeled partner literally loses his or her identity in the eyes of the other. We tend to want to keep confirming this label in our own heads. So, for example, if you label your husband as selfish, you will be on a mission to look for reasons why he is selfish—after all, isn't that what you convinced yourself? It is incredibly ironic how so many people resort to labeling their partners, when they themselves resent being labeled!

There is another point about labeling in relationships. Labels can often start out as playful statements. We have heard the expression "Many a truth is spoken in jest." The playfulness of a label can easily turn toxic. For example, Scott may first begin labeling Jennifer as a shopaholic in a playful way. He may kid her about how she is solely responsible for supporting their local retail economy, and Jennifer may tease Scott about being a couch potato. But, if Scott loses his job three years later, Jennifer's spending may be perceived in a more distorted toxic way and Scott's retreat to the couch may also be viewed far more negatively. Labels can be very toxic even when followed by "I was only kidding."

#5: The Blame Game

Walt is furious with Gail, his wife of twenty-five years. He is beside himself with anger at Gail for her sexual shutdown of the past seven years. Gail blames Walt for becoming overly consumed with his work, just like her father was when she was growing up. Walt also blames Gail for her excessive credit card bills and for lying to him. Gail blames Walt for not being able or willing to discuss finances or any other issues with her. Walt has been waiting for Gail to fix herself for twenty-five years and is baffled why she just can't change to make the marriage better. Gail can't wait for Walt to finally "get it" and to become a more understanding husband.

What a mess! It can be very tempting to believe that your relationship problems are the fault of your partner. After all, if you think it is completely your partner's fault then that absolves you of any fault or liability. But a relationship's problems are rarely exclusively the fault of one partner. It really does take two to make or break a relationship. While it might feel natural to blame your partner for your relationship problems, this strategy usually makes things worse.

It is best to focus on the person you have any control over—yourself—and to teach yourself how to think and react differently when facing relationship conflicts. After working personally with hundreds of couples, I can tell you that blaming the other partner does not resolve conflicts.

It amazes me how many separated and divorced people I encounter who rigidly perceive themselves as "relationship victims." We have all heard these "victims" tell their story about how the death of the relationship was not their fault, displacing the blame onto their former partner. This sure gets old! And, sadly, partners who fall into this toxic thought pattern leave their divorce lawyers with much to gain.

The words "if" and "only" are red flags in the Blame Game. You will know that your relationship is suffering from toxic blaming if you or your partner make statements like "It's not my fault. If only you would stop doing this, we'd be okay," or "If she hadn't opened her big mouth . . . ," or "If you were a normal person, you would see that you're emotionally closed."

Blame is about denial. An extreme example of denial on the part of the blaming partner can be found by looking at abusive relationships. How often have you heard about the abuser blaming his partner for his actions? This can take the form of "You made me hit you!" or "I would not have hit you if you did not make me so upset." A seemingly less aggressive but just as twisted form of denial is an initial apology followed by "but" and then the blame. "I'm sorry I'm late, but if you hadn't asked me to wash the car, I would have been on time."

Blame is toxic because it causes one partner to feel shamed by the other. A couple I worked with, Rick and Sally, painfully illustrate this point. When Sally blamed all of their financial problems on Rick's disastrous investments, he told me, "I feel so stupid and worthless."

When I asked Sally, "How do you feel knowing Rick feels worthless?" she quickly said, "Oh, I don't want him to feel worthless. I just want him to leave the investing to me from now on so we won't have this problem anymore." I believed Sally when she said that she didn't intend to belittle Rick for his mistake. However, the outcome was that he did feel belittled and worthless.

Blame contributes to The Three-D Effect because it focuses responsibility on the partners, not on the problem. We blame our partners because we are seeking an answer to the question "Who did it?" rather than "What can we do about it?" Blame communicates the desire to punish. All this does is cause the other partner to shut down. Sadly, toxic thoughts of blame lead to missed opportunities to resolve the conflict. Distorted, toxic thoughts about blame suggest that one partner is responsible and the other is not. All this does is create further resentment, prolong the conflict, and set the stage for future conflicts.

I am often asked, "But what if it really is his (her) fault?"

I'm not saying it is always fifty-fifty. Your partner may have forgotten to do something, overlooked something, or gotten distracted. But how you think and react are your responsibility—not his or hers. If you stop focusing on who's to blame, then the focus is on the issue, and issues are much easier to work through than blame.

#6: Emotional Short-Circuit

Stacy, whose father left the family when she was a child, has problems with her siblings. Recently, Stacy learned that the father she's never known has a terminal illness and wants to meet her. Two of Stacy's sisters are pressuring her to meet him while her brother says he won't speak to any of them if they decide to see him. Kevin, Stacy's husband of nine years, wants to be supportive and help her deal with this difficult decision. Not knowing how to act, Kevin reaches to hold Stacy as they lie together in bed reading. Stacy tries hard to relax and accept Kevin's gesture, but she tenses up because she views Kevin's embrace as a quick step to sex rather than just an attempt to comfort her. Kevin feels Stacey stiffen and thinks, For God's sake, I'm just trying to help. *Kevin abruptly pulls away and then tells Stacy that she has too much baggage for him to handle.*

Emotional Short-Circuit occurs when one partner convinces him- or herself that his or her partner's emotions can't be "handled." Typically, this occurs with a partner who has great difficulty relating to the emotions or emotional issues of the other partner. In this case, the thoughts may be *All she does is carry on* or *He's got no right to be that upset.*

Individuals who Emotionally Short-Circuit sometimes perceive the expression of emotions as a sign of weakness. Partners prone to Emotional Short-Circuiting want to genuinely help their partners but become frustrated when they themselves feel helpless. A partner who emotionally short-circuits can unknowingly leave their partner feeling devalued.

Emotional Short-Circuiting frequently leads to one partner giving the emotional partner the "silent treatment." In this case the partner who short-circuits feels that ignoring his or her partner is the most effective way to deal with negative thoughts and feelings. The silent treatment strategy is toxic in its own right. It is a passive-aggressive strategy that is often hurtful and rarely productive. By passive-aggressive, I am referring to partners who have difficulty directly expressing themselves, so they illustrate their feelings (usually anger, and the underlying hurt or disappointment) in more indirect ways, such as not talking or slamming doors.

Emotional Short-Circuiting is a major problem in relationships. Like other toxic thoughts, it is a judgmental way to express yourself. The tendency to impose such rigid expectations and judgments on a partner is paradoxical when we consider that a relationship grants partners the freedom to be vulnerable.

Occasionally, we hear in the news about a person who suddenly discovers that her spouse or partner has a shockingly secret life (he's a sexual offender, has a major criminal record, or never mentioned a wife and kids to his other wife in another state). In most cases, however, each partner can get a pretty good idea of who the other is and how he (she) reacts during the early stages of the relationship. In other words, you get what you sign up for. This being the case, if the Emotional Short-Circuit is not dealt with, it usually happens over and over again, because the party who short-circuits never grows to accommodate his or her partner's emotional reactions.

#7: Overactive Imagination

Lisa, Jerry's wife of seven years, comes home an hour late from a nursing department Christmas party at the suburban hospital where she works. Jerry's Overactive Imagination, fueled by his deep-seated belief that he is not an adequate enough provider, leads him to conclude that Lisa is having an affair with a "rich doctor." Jerry asks Lisa why she is late, and she tells him that she got into a conversation with the other nurses about some outrageous new nursing policies. Jerry has a hard time believing Lisa, even in the face of her clear warmth and enthusiasm about seeing him.

Partners prone to an Overactive Imagination tend to have trouble controlling their anxiety. Examples of Overactive Imagination toxic thoughts include *She must be having an affair, He probably had an accident,* and *He's going to leave me.* When partners feel insecure or have low self-esteem, Overactive Imagination can easily take over.

Overactive Imagination results from a need for control. Anxious people tend to need to believe that they are in control. Doubts that fuel the Overactive Imagination of a partner can lead him or her to feel out of control. And so it goes—the vicious cycle of Overactive Imagination. The more anxiety one partner experiences toward the other, the more the anxious party tries to convince himself that she (he) is "right." Ironically, the anxious party then often uses faulty, erroneous, accusatory explanations to fill in the blanks.

When one partner's expectations for a certain type of response from the other partner are not met, toxic thoughts are easily triggered. Partners then harmfully (and unknowingly) rely on their anxiety to give them answers, like *She must have been in a car accident. What if she's dead! Oh, my God, what will I ever do without her!* This is similar to what occurs in Catastrophic Conclusions, but there is a major difference. In the case of Catastrophic Conclusions, one partner exaggerates the consequences of actual events. With Overactive Imagination, thoughts are not based in reality at all.

Suppose you're the wife of the man who thinks that, because you're half an hour late, you're dead. At first, when the relationship is new, you may be touched by his concern. You may appreciate it. But over time, many partners of catastrophizers tell me that they feel burdened, stressed, and annoyed by the conclusions their partners draw. Catastrophic Conclusions create distance between couples, and if you're distant, you're not able to communicate with or appreciate one another.

#8: Head Game Gamble

Allen thinks Linda, his wife of twenty years, has a hidden agenda when she is affectionate and kind to him. He thinks, I know how she operates. *She wants to visit her sister for the weekend, so she is just trying to warm me up. Allen interprets Linda's kindness as evidence that she is manipulating him. He loses sight of the behavior at hand because he is assuming that she has ulterior motives.*

Head games are a particularly common, even accepted practice among people who date, especially when the relationship is new. *I'll wait until Wednesday to call so she doesn't think I'm too anxious to see her,* or *If he asks me out, I'll say no, so he realizes he should call sooner for Saturday night* are common strategies. Dating people play these games because they feel vulnerable and insecure. We've all been there. But most couples hope and strive to get past the head games.

Most couples do, in fact, get beyond the typical dating head games but as the relationship becomes more established, a new kind of head game starts. Head Game Gamble occurs when partners believe they know each other so well that they *think* they can "read each other's minds." Many people erroneously believe that years together automatically means they will know what the other feels, thinks, or intends. The Head Game Gamble often involves one partner believing the other partner's specific behaviors are directed at him or her. One partner thinks *He woke up early and cleaned the kitchen to rub it in that I don't do enough* or *She's staying out late to pay me back because I didn't make her dinner.*

Head Game Gambles tend to occur with partners who misinterpret the actions of the other partner. (This differs from Overactive Imagination, where misperceptions are based on things that have not even happened.)

The misinterpretations that occur in the Head Game Gamble result from inaccurate interpretations of your partner's behaviors. While all toxic thoughts involve distortions, the Head Game Gamble involves incorrect assumptions in response to your partner's actions. I call this distortion the Head Game Gamble because assuming hidden meanings in your partner's behaviors is like betting in a game of black jack—you may "win" once in a while by outsmarting the dealer, but more often than not you'll lose.

The Head Game Gambler may think *She only had sex with me because she did not want me to be mad about her shopping spree* or *She is sleeping with our sick child just to get out of having sex with me* or *He only brought me flowers because. . . .*

Head Game Gamblers assume that their partners have negative intentions. I'm not saying that the other partner is always an angel. In fact, the other partner may very well engage in some manipulative actions from time to time. The problem with the Head Game Gamble is the excessive degree to which one party perceives that the other has ulterior motives. Head Game Gamblers have low self-esteem and have a hard time believing that their partners truly value them. Since they don't adequately value themselves, they question their value in the eyes of their partners. This surfaces in their questioning of the other partners' actions and motives.

#9: Disillusionment Doom

Though many of her friends envy her upscale lifestyle, Terri wishes that she and John could go back to the days when they lived in their

apartment and everything they owned could fit in the backseat of
their Volkswagen. The money they now have in the bank feels mean-
ingless to Terri, as does their huge house. She thinks John has sold out
to the hustle and bustle of corporate life, something she never thought
he would do.

Couples often become sidetracked from real relationship issues,
like trust and intimacy, because they have idealized expectations and
fantasies of their partners. This leads to the inevitable feeling of being
let down. One partner feels betrayed or disappointed by the other
because he or she has not lived up to certain standards or expectations.

The Dalai Lama has written much about happiness. He writes,
"All beings are seeking happiness." His recommendations for *finding*
happiness are to be grateful for what we have and to give to others.
Yet in our society, we are brought up to find someone who will *make*
us happy. When we buy into these rigid expectations about our partners and then they don't make us happy (because who could?)
Disillusionment Doom sets in.

Examples of thoughts of people with Disillusionment Doom
include *He wasn't this stubborn when I married him* (Yes, he probably
was) or *She's really putting on weight* (Well, you would too after having two children) or *I thought she would want to stay home with the kids
and quit her job* (Yes, but didn't she tell you how important her career
is to her?).

Many people have unrealistic expectations for their relationships
to begin with and become disappointed by their partners' personality
traits, physical appearance, or habits. Couples often begin to argue
about spending, bathroom habits, or personality traits, which
obstructs their ability to work out their real issues.

Since we usually have a good sense of who our partners are when we
meet them, I find it interesting how often I hear Disillusionment
Doomers say, "We had little in common" or again, my favorite, "We just
drifted apart." I don't buy into this logic. I believe that "we just drifted
apart" is really just the outward expression of secretly held thoughts of
Disillusionment Doom. In fact, my colleagues and I agree that about
seventy percent of problems in relationships are never "solved," rather,
they are accepted and addressed. Thus Disillusionment Doom, like all

toxic thoughts, is based more on unrealistic expectations and distortions than on reality.

Disillusionment Doom toxic thinkers have a low tolerance for change in their partners. Consider Seth and Helen. Helen thought, *I figured that with Seth being in the military, he would always be structured and predictable. I can't believe that he now wants to be a musician.*

I have also found a subgroup of Disillusionment Doom toxic thinkers who like acquiring new material possessions. They want the latest new gadgets, cars, and accessories. Not surprisingly, people who easily get bored of things tend to have extramarital affairs as a means of adding a sense of newness to their perceived drab and overly routine lives.

Suffice it to say, Disillusionment Doom, like all other toxic thoughts, can lurk silently in the minds of partners and can cause major damage to the relationship if it is not dealt with.

TO SUM IT ALL UP

AS YOU WERE reading about the nine toxic thought patterns that ruin relationships, you may have had one of those "aha!" moments, when you suddenly saw yourself or your relationship. That's very common. But you may need more time to understand which pattern or patterns you need help changing. You may need to "catch" yourself in a toxic moment. You may need to review these toxic patterns over the course of the next week or two.

The rest of this book focuses on strategies for tuning in and talking back to your toxic thoughts. They *can* be disputed and addressed, as you'll soon see. Keep in mind that these toxic thoughts result in The Three-D Effect—Distraction, Distance, and Disconnect—and can lead to many other problems as well. But remember there is hope, and you don't have to go to a marriage counselor or a therapist to get it (unless, of course, you choose to). Now let's look at how to begin to win the fight.

4
Your MAP
Back to Love

NOW YOU KNOW what toxic thoughts are and how destructive they are to relationships. You understand how toxic thoughts trap you in a rigid mindset that weakens your ability to talk to, argue with, and resolve conflicts with your partner.

Here's the good news: I believe—with great passion and conviction—that *if you can think yourself into conflict and out of love; you can think your way out of conflict and back into love.* More important than my belief, however, is what I've seen as a couples' counselor. I've seen hundreds of couples in trouble or on the brink of separation step up, use my strategies, and think themselves back to love.

You, your partner, and your relationship will never be completely or totally free of toxic thoughts. Remember, it's human nature to think negatively and even toxically at times. But you can prevent toxic thinking from damaging your relationship and disrupting your communication. This I can practically guarantee.

HOW MAP CAN HELP

IN FACT, I can even give you a MAP back to love.

Actually, **MAP** stands for **Mindfulness, Alternatives**, and **Practice**, an easy-to-follow approach to ridding your relationship of toxic thoughts. First, you have to recognize, or be mindful, that you are having toxic thoughts. Next, you need to develop alternative explanations for your toxic thoughts. When you develop more realistic interpretations of your partner's words and actions, you will be empowered to dispute your toxic thoughts and replace them with healthier and more helpful thoughts. Finally, you've got to practice. Though we all want to change instantly and we all want better relationships overnight, the truth is that it takes time and practice. No matter who you are and what your relationship is like, it took you time to toxify; it will take you time to detoxify. The more you practice both mindfulness and alternatives, the stronger the improvements in your relationship. It takes work to create positive changes. In the words of David Starr Jordan, a noted scientist and educator, "Wisdom is knowing what to do next; virtue is doing it."

If you put it all together—Mindfulness, Alternatives, and Practice—you have the key to creating permanent trust, intimacy, and honest communication in your relationship. You have a personal MAP back to love. Pretty simple. But don't be fooled. MAP's effects on relationships are often quite powerful—powerful enough to bring many couples I know back from The Three-D Effect and even, at times, from the brink of separation.

Each piece of your MAP feeds the others in a positive and reinforcing way. As the picture below shows, these three steps occur within a circle.

Mindfulness, becoming aware of and responsible for your toxic thoughts, leads you to develop alternatives to dispute, control, and eliminate them. The more you practice, the more mindful you will

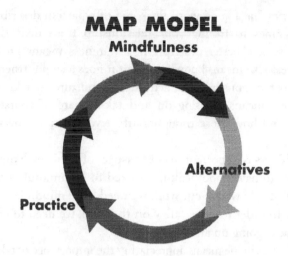

MAP MODEL
Mindfulness

Alternatives

Practice

become and the faster you will be able to eliminate toxic thoughts from your relationship.

Let's discuss mindfulness and then I'll introduce four simple steps you need to take to achieve it in your relationship.

RELATIONSHIP MINDFULNESS HELPS RELATIONSHIPS THRIVE

YOU MAY BE wondering about this mindfulness business. What is it, and how do you become and stay mindful? What does mindfulness have to do with toxic thinking?

Here's more good news. By reading the first three chapters of this book, you're already well on your way to becoming more mindful about your relationship and how it can be threatened or ruined by toxic thinking. Such mindfulness is critical if a relationship is going to thrive. You've already taken the first step to a healthier and happier relationship and you didn't even know it!

When I spoke about mindfulness to a group of couples, a woman raised her hand and said, "Isn't mindfulness just a new-age, trendy way to say 'aware'? Aren't you telling us we need to pay attention to what we're thinking?"

"Awareness" is a good word for some of what I'm describing, but when it comes to freeing your relationship from toxic thinking, mindfulness is a better description. Awareness means knowledge. Mindfulness also means knowledge, but it goes a step further, implying a deeper responsibility to acquire and nurture that knowledge. Mindfulness means focusing on and taking care of yourself, your thoughts, and how those thoughts affect your actions toward your partner.

Mindfulness is important in every aspect of our lives. Think about it. In order to have good health, we need to be mindful of how our bodies feel. To do well in our work we need to be mindful of our performance. In order to drive safely on the road, we need to be mindful of what is going on around us.

Mindfulness in life means appreciating the importance of taking care of things over time. Taking care of things over time is called maintenance. This being the case, we must be mindful to maintain our appreciation of all that we give and receive in our lives, including how we think about and treat our intimate partners. Relationship mindfulness means creating, cultivating, and nurturing an ongoing passion and conviction to honor your partner and your relationship. This truly is a big deal. An intimate connection with another human being is an honor. I know it can be hard for couples in distress to appreciate this fact. I know that at times your partnership can feel like a jail sentence. But once you are free of toxic thinking, you will be able to appreciate the specialness of your relationship far more. You won't be so bogged down in negativity. You will have the energy and the renewed spirit to maintain and grow your relationship. I promise you that relationship mindfulness will spur you to do this. I also promise you that relationships do not survive on autopilot. The fact is that when you don't maintain and nurture intimacy, your relationship will be consumed by your disappointment, your unrealistic expectations, and the stresses of life.

FOUR SIMPLE STEPS TO RELATIONSHIP MINDFULNESS

HERE ARE FOUR simple steps you will take in your mindful approach to eliminating toxic thinking from your relationship:

Step One: Listen to Your Toxic Thoughts

Because you're reading this, you've probably already begun to catch yourself thinking toxic thoughts. Maybe you need more time to tune in and focus on your toxic thinking. That's fine. You simply need to be listening for toxic thinking and that will be easy now that you know what the nine types are. You *will* become aware of them. You don't have to meditate or go to a quiet room. All you really have to do is pay attention to your thoughts, especially when you realize you're thinking about your partner. Naturally, your direct interactions with your partner will spur you to think about him or her. Therefore, a good time to check in and hear what you're thinking is when you're with him or her.

But it can be just as effective to tune in during those quiet times, when you're in the shower, walking the dog, or commuting to work. Just listen to what you're telling yourself about your partner and your relationship. Remember, you self-talk all day long. Naturally, not all of your thoughts will be about your partner, but a very good number of them will be and you need to hear what you're saying to yourself.

Ashanti told me that she couldn't believe the amount of internal chatter she had about her fiancé Jackson. "There I was walking my dog, using the pooper scooper to pick up the mess, and thinking how I wanted to put the contents on his front porch. Though I knew I was upset with Jackson for refusing to set a firm date for our wedding, until I tuned in I didn't realize how much more upset I was than I was letting on to him. I was stunned at the amount of time I spent thinking toxic thoughts about him."

You may not recognize your toxic thoughts as they occur in "real time," such as when you're in the middle of an argument. You may just be used to thinking, *I'm angry and that is all there is to it.* That's okay. When you're new to this process, remember you can always go back and rethink things. After an argument with your partner, prompt yourself with questions like *What was I telling myself about the way Peter was acting?* or *What was I thinking right before I told Jenny that I couldn't take it anymore?*

The most important thing isn't to catch yourself immediately but to catch yourself eventually. (It's not a contest; it's a process.)

Here are five tips for zooming in on toxic thoughts:

1. Commit to listening to your thoughts for at least a week. You may be catching yourself thinking toxic thoughts frequently, but many people need a good chunk of time, at least several days, to train themselves to listen. For most of your life, you haven't paid close attention to your idle self-talk. It can take time to create this new habit.

2. Give yourself a reminder. Some people find it helpful to tape a note to the bathroom mirror or their computer that says, "Pay attention" or "Remember to listen," just to remind themselves to listen in on their self-talk. One of my clients wore a piece of purple ribbon around her wrist to remind her to listen in. She would look at it and think, Why am I wearing this? and then quickly realize, Okay, I remember, and listen to herself.

3. Keep a small notebook in your purse, briefcase, or pocket. It can be helpful to see your toxic thoughts in black and white, even just for a day or two. Like many people I've worked with, you may be stunned at the sheer volume of toxic thoughts that you didn't even know you were having.

4. Listen for the language of toxic thinking. As you now know, toxic thinking encourages the use of certain words and phrases such as "always" and "never" (All or Nothing), "should" (*Should* Bomb), "I can't handle" (Emotional Short-Circuit), "she's going to . . ." (Catastrophic Conclusions), "if only" (Blame Game), and "he didn't do this when I married him" (Disillusionment Doom).

5. Don't make any judgments about yourself or your partner. This is just about tuning in and listening. This is not about catching yourself being a bad husband, wife, or partner. This is simply about becoming more aware of the toxic thoughts you're automatically telling yourself about your partner.

Step Two: Pay Attention to How You Feel Physically

Tuning in to your body, particularly to your physical reactions to your thoughts, will help keep you mindful of toxic thoughts as they occur. The link between our minds and bodies is well recognized. We talk about "gut feelings," tension in our heads and stomachs, and even how some people can be a "pain in the butt." While many people are initially surprised to discover that their thoughts trigger physical reactions or sensations, it's a fact that they do. Researchers in many fields, both medical and psychological, have clearly shown that we have the ability to feel calm, stressed, sad, angry, happy, or any other emotion in response to our thoughts.

Again, you don't have to light candles and meditate, though you certainly can if you want to. My point is that cultivating relationship mindfulness really isn't all that difficult and doesn't require any major life changes. You simply need to pay attention to your body. Many couples suffering from The Three-D Effect will often feel physically uncomfortable just at the sight of their partner.

Gina told me that every night her whole body would tense up at the sound of her husband's key in the door. Danny was an alcoholic and usually stopped by the neighborhood tavern before coming home for dinner angry and agitated.

Gina: "I would literally grit my teeth and clench my fists for the battle about to unfold. He was always mad. Dinner was late. Dinner was early. There was always something. . . . After Danny started to go to AA and even after he'd been sober for one whole year, I still found myself tensing up when I heard him coming home. It was like I had trained myself to tense up in preparation for his behavior, but then never untrained myself when he stopped drinking."

Gina's experience is not unlike that of the work of the famous Russian scientist Pavlov, who presented a dog with a ringing bell paired with a steak. After doing this repeatedly, Pavlov found over time that the dog salivated upon just hearing the bell. Similarly, we develop strong associations and expectations about our partners. It's amazing how our bodies can be surprisingly reliable barometers of our thoughts and feelings.

This is why I urge you to pay attention to your body. For example, you may notice that your neck is killing you or your heart beats more strongly as soon as your husband walks into the room (*He's probably going to start blaming me again*). Or your wife walks in and starts to slam cabinets and you instantly get a burning sensation in your stomach (*She's always mad about something*). These are prime opportunities to connect what you're feeling in your body to what's going on in your mind. Toxic thoughts don't just come and go. They stick and they often make you sick. So when you start to feel clenched or achy, tune into what you're thinking. Chances are you will catch yourself having toxic thoughts about your partner. (Even if they're not about your partner, you will still benefit from tuning in and finding out what or who is causing your stress.)

Tuning into physical cues from your body is an important step in cultivating relationship mindfulness. Often, your body knows what your mind is thinking before you're aware of it.

BODY CUES FOR TOXIC THOUGHTS		
sweaty palms	lethargy	ringing ears
tense jaw	shaking limbs	nausea
headache	quavering voice	insomnia
stomachache	blurred vision	neck or backache
shortness of breath	loud voice	fatigue
grinding teeth	clenching fists	dizziness

Here are two tips that can help you tune into your body for physical clues to your toxic thinking:

1. **Know what being tense and being relaxed feels like.** You may think this is unnecessary. Who doesn't know what it feels like to be stressed out? But many of us are so tense so much of the time that we are used to being that way. Being tense or having a headache can begin to seem normal. It can be hard to tell when you're tensing up if you spend quite a bit of your day stressed out. Before you go to bed or after work, take a few moments and relax. Either sitting up or lying down, acknowledge and relax

each part of your body. Here's how my client Patrick taught himself to do this: "I simply go through my whole body and say, 'Now my knees are relaxed. And there are my thighs. Am I glad to see those hard working thighs relax. . . . ' When my whole body is relaxed, I try to take note of how it feels not to be tense. I stay that way for a few minutes. Then I tense my whole body and hold it for a few seconds. Then I release it. That really shows me the difference between tension and relaxation."

2. **When you note your body is tense, acknowledge the tension.** Ask yourself, "Why am I holding my breath? Why are my shoulders so sore? What am I thinking about?" Allow your focus to shift from your body to your thoughts. This also works in reverse. If you find yourself having a toxic thought about your partner, note the effect it's having on your body. It's important to be aware of the physical toll that toxic thinking takes on your body. Think about it; if you tense your shoulders every time you're thinking, *He should know I need a hug,* you're going to have very sore shoulders by the end of your first year together!

Step Three: Determine Your Triggers for Toxic Thinking

We all have triggers for toxic thinking, particularly around common stressors like sex, money, kids, and in-laws. These are the specific situations or times when we are particularly prone to toxic thoughts because of an emotional investment or just stress and worry. It's important to recognize what these triggers are so you'll be aware when you're most at risk for toxic thinking.

For Meg and Steve, a toxic thought trigger was childrearing.

Meg: "After our first son was born, Steve and I fought about everything; the right way to change a diaper, the right way to burp him, the right way to wash bottles. You name it and we argued about it. It got to the point where I felt Steve was constantly criticizing me. He would say, 'Let me show you how I would do it,' and I would think, *He thinks I'm stupid* or *He doesn't think I can handle motherhood.*"

Steve, on the other hand, felt shut out by Meg.

Steve: "I would think, *She doesn't want my input as a dad. I'm just a money machine to her, just a way to have a longer maternity leave.* I felt like she didn't respect me or care about my opinions. It was a tough time for us. Every time we tried to talk about it, we degenerated into a screaming match of 'You always discount me' and 'You don't care about my opinion.' I think we were both scared when I suggested seeing a counselor because we knew we really needed it."

Fortunately, Meg and Steve were able to recognize that adjusting to their new role as parents was a stressor that triggered toxic thinking. Once she was able to recognize that her thoughts on this issue had become toxic, Meg was able to step back and rethink her and Steve's positions. She went from *He doesn't think I can handle it* to *He just loves his son and wants to be a part of the experience.*

Steve was able to step back and rethink the situation as well. He went from *Meg thinks I'm just the money maker* to *Motherhood is a powerful experience for Meg. She's feeling her way as a mom and, because she's not secure yet, interprets my input as criticism.*

Here are three guidelines to help you identify your toxic thought triggers:

1. **Look for the Patterns.** In step one, zooming in on your toxic thoughts, I suggested keeping a notebook so you can write down your toxic thoughts. This is a great way to see if there are one or two particular areas that are triggers for you. You might, for example, notice that your toxic thoughts surround money or your in-laws. Many people are surprised to discover how many toxic thoughts end up clustering around one area. (No wonder you're stressed out!)

2. **Keep Track of Your Arguments.** Do you and you spouse have a particular hot button issue, like sex, socializing, or household chores? If you do, chances are that a recurring battle area is a toxic trigger. If you find yourself having an argument about a

common theme, pay particular attention to your thoughts; you will probably be having toxic thoughts.

3. **Realize That Your Stressors Will Change.** Right now, your husband's job may cause you to think toxically (*He should know I hate when he works late*). Later, however, it could become money (*All he cares about is making more money*). Relationships often experience stressful periods. You may be caring for young children at one point in your relationship, and for your aging parents at another. Know that staying on top of one stressor doesn't guarantee there won't be others that need your attention.

A toxic thought trigger can commonly be more than just a common stressor like a lack of money or sex. Many times, what sends us into toxic thinking mode is one of our personal issues, or "baggage" as it's more commonly called.

Most of us don't like to deal with our past issues. Believe me, I do this for a living and even I hate to deal with my past baggage. Why? No one likes to feel past hurts or recognize mistakes. We're all human. That's just natural. But I do try to acknowledge my baggage because I know it's better for me if I do. I know that when I don't have a sense of how those issues predispose me to certain toxic thoughts, it is like walking in the dark—I keep bumping into the same issues without any warning. What I said earlier really is true, "What you resist will persist."

For better or worse, what we learn about intimacy is heavily influenced by our past relationships and our families. Most of us are oblivious to this. For example, families who expressively show affection and warmth will shape different expectations and perceptions than families who are reserved with their emotions. People who grow up with a parent or parents who are emotionally withdrawn will be unwittingly taught "rules" about showing feelings that are different from people raised in families that freely express emotions. If you grew up in this withdrawn family environment, you may be prone to All or Nothing or Emotional Short-Circuit toxic thoughts about an insecure partner, such as *He is always smothering me. He's out of control.*

But just as you can discover common stressors that may trigger toxic thinking, you can discover what past issues you may have that are impairing your thinking now. You need to become mindful about your old baggage, and one of the easiest ways is to recognize the symptoms. If the people closest to you continually react to you in the same ways and you hear the same negative feedback (overly jumping to conclusions, or being overly controlling), maybe it is time to go look in the mirror. This isn't about being self-critical or blaming your parents for feeling crummy now. It's about understanding yourself on a deeper level so you can improve your intimate relationship. I talk about emotional ghosts in much more detail in Chapter Seven.

Step Four: Remain Calm—Don't Go Toxic

A big problem with toxic thinking is that it can trigger toxic feelings, such as anger, frustration, and resentment. In Chapter Two, I asked you to tune into your feelings as a way to gauge the extent to which your relationship may be suffering from toxic thinking. Now it's time to learn specifically how toxic thoughts actually create, activate, and escalate those negative, relationship-bashing feelings. Let's consider the immense power of feelings.

Our feelings are manipulated by advertisements, politicians, our children, our parents, our coworkers, and even our pets (remember how you felt when you walked in and saw your cat's hair balls on the new rug?). So are we really just passive beings whose fate is at the mercy of people who can influence our feelings?

Not necessarily. Have you ever talked yourself out of buying something you could not afford? Have you ever wanted to scream or punch someone in public but held your tongue or your fist? Or how about the time you counted to ten instead of going completely ballistic when your child "decorated" your new couch with fruit punch? In all these cases, you thought about things differently and you created a different way of thinking, which changed your feelings and led to a different outcome. Your feelings did not just arise out of the blue and you did not just cave in to them. That takes discipline and strength. That's being a grown-up.

Sadly, too many of us do not apply such discipline when we interact with our intimate partners. Our insecurities and past baggage cause hot buttons and triggers that get set off. Unfortunately, we really buy into the "You made me feel…" myth with our intimate partners. But we don't have to go there. *By controlling our toxic thinking, we can control our feelings.*

THE PAYOFF

As you become more mindful of toxic thinking, an amazing transformation will occur. You will realize that you *do* have a choice about your feelings when it comes to your partner—a choice not to feel the anger, rejection, or frustration that toxic thinking inevitably causes you to feel. Sure, giving in to your toxic thoughts is a lot easier in the short term, and it can even feel good. But you and your partner have to live with the long-term consequences. Realize that when you take the bait of toxic thoughts, your feelings immediately spiral out of control. For example, Peter was quick to take his All or Nothing toxic thought, *She never initiates sex with me,* and jump to the Catastrophic Conclusion, *She must be having an affair.* This conclusion sent him into a spiral of despair and resentment. By not being mindful of his toxic thinking, his feelings are probably not the reality of his relationship.

I like to think of mindfulness as the opposite of toxic thinking. Toxic thinking is automatic, habitlike, one-sided, rigid, and destructive to relationships. Mindfulness, on the other hand, is purposeful and fluid; it promotes acceptance and empathy, the emotional glue that bonds partners.

When you have an automatic toxic thought like *He should know I need a break,* your emotional response to that toxic thought is also automatic, and it's most likely anger, frustration, disappointment, or another unpleasant emotion. In order to remain mindful, you've got to keep yourself from getting angry or frustrated. You've got to keep your cool. Becoming mindful in this way will empower you to move beyond a primitive response, like anger, and use your feelings in a more constructive way. Just because you experience toxic thoughts does not mean you have to feel what they are telling you to feel.

Here are three suggestions for remaining calm and avoiding toxic feelings and actions:

1. **Talk Yourself Out of It.** If you can talk yourself into it, you can talk yourself out of it. Say to yourself, *I'm feeling mad/sad/rejected/hurt because of a toxic thought that may not reflect reality.* Then ask yourself, *Do I want to have control over my thoughts or do I want them to control me?* Of course you want to control your thoughts. Maybe you do have the right to be angry or annoyed at your partner. The problem is that if you act toxically, your ability to discuss the issues becomes seriously impaired.

2. **Give Yourself a Mantra.** Keeping yourself from feeling a toxic feeling *can* be as simple as recognizing that you're having a toxic thought and repeating a simple self-talk phrase, or mantra, like *Okay, slow down.* Repeating short phrases over and over again helps you create a new thinking habit. Remember, you thought your way into frustration and unhappiness with your partner, so you have to practice thinking your way out of it. A little phrase like *Okay, this not at all horrible, Calm down, this may not be what it seems,* or *Wait a minute, is this toxic thinking talking?* can act as a gentle reminder to remain mindful and avoid toxic thinking.

3. **Breathe Deeply.** When you catch yourself having a toxic thought, make a point to *breathe deeply.* Yes, it's simple, but simple is good. Deep breaths will calm and slow you down. The next time you're upset or angry, notice your breath. You're probably going to find it stuck in your chest or throat. Our natural inclination is to stop breathing or breathe in a shallow manner when stressed. As you'll see, it's hard to remain clenched and toxic when you are breathing deeply. Dr. Andrew Weil, the famous Harvard-trained physician, views breathing as "the master key to self-healing." Herbert Benson actually coined the term "relaxation response," which was based on breathing and mindfulness techniques. And then there's Vincent, a sixty-three-year-old client of mine whose wife was ready to walk out on him. Talk about The Three-D Effect! This couple had barely spoken for over a year. A self-described "old-fashioned guy who doesn't go in for any new-age hoo-ha," Vince was quick to dismiss my advice to breathe deeply when he became aware of his toxic thinking. But because his wife really was

about to walk out if he didn't at least try to improve their communication, Vincent began to breathe deeply at the first sign of toxic thinking. Only a week later, Vincent was a convert. "I can't believe how much better I feel with this breathing," he said. "I never realized how much I was holding my breath all the time. I really do feel better. I really am able to calm myself down before it's too late." I'll never forget Vincent's smile as he quipped that an "old dog" really can be taught new tricks! If Vincent can make breath a positive force in his battle against toxic thinking, you can too. (See the box below for the proper breathing technique.)

■

HOW TO BREATHE FOR MINDFULNESS

1. Breathe in deeply through your nose to a count of four.

2. As you breathe in, allow your stomach and chest to expand with air.

3. Hold this breath for a count of four.

4. Exhale slowly to a count of seven or eight.

5. Repeat at least three times, or until you feel calm.

■

TO SUM IT ALL UP

YEARS AGO THERE was a movie called *The Blob*, about a blob of gook that fell from outer space and started swallowing people whole. The more people it swallowed, the bigger it became. Unchecked toxic thinking is like the blob. You now have four very simple, yet very result-oriented steps to help you become more mindful so you *can* do something about your toxic thinking.

Here's what you need to remember: Mindfulness is crucial to the survival of your relationship. Mindfulness allows you to deal with the inevitable disappointments, frustrations, and hurts from your partner, and your partner to deal with those from you. If you are not in control of yourself and your thoughts, your impatience, anger, and other toxic feelings will eventually erode your communication and even the relationship itself.

In order to achieve relationship mindfulness and overcome your toxic thinking, you must take four simple steps:

- ▶ Listen to Your Thoughts
- ▶ Pay Attention to How You Feel Physically
- ▶ Determine Your Triggers for Toxic Thinking
- ▶ Remain Calm—Choose Not to Feel Toxic Feelings

The great thing about these steps is that you don't have to change anything except your thinking. Give yourself a week or two to practice being mindful. I promise you, once you create the habit of listening to toxic thoughts, you will be amazed to find out what you've been telling yourself about your partner and your relationship.

5

The Better
Alternative to
Toxic Thinking

ONCE YOU'RE ABLE to be mind-
ful of your toxic thoughts without feeling angry, neglected, or any of
the other negative feelings I've discussed, you're ready to take the
next step in MAP—alternatives.

Breaking out of the toxic thinking habit means you must find
alternatives (new and better ways to look at your partner's words or
actions) to your negative and destructive thoughts. Remember, it's
not the situation but the *interpretation* of the situation that makes the
difference between happy and unhappy couples. You can choose to
interpret the actions or words of your partner toxically (unrealistic-
ally) or you can choose to interpret them nontoxically (realistically).

I'm not encouraging you to put on rose-colored glasses and ignore
the things your partner does that bug you. Far from it! Developing
alternatives is about learning to change your thoughts so that you can
see your partner in a fair, balanced, and encouraging way.

Fortunately, the theory that we can change and shape our own thinking has been rigorously studied in the field of cognitive therapy. Cognitive therapists show clients how they can systematically train themselves to think their way out of depression, anxiety, anger, and other problematic emotions. The key is to be aware that thoughts cause feelings and that by changing the flawed underlying thinking, you can change how you feel.

Once you have this new perspective, you will be able to truly communicate with your partner and work through your issues. Being mindful and preventing your own irrational, toxic baggage from distorting your view of your partner is crucial to healthy communication. When you start using alternative ways of thinking about your relationship, your toxic thinking days are numbered.

I ask you to keep this in mind: Your relationship perspective leads to your relationship reality.

Clearly, if your partner's behaviors are repeatedly vindictive, manipulative, or abusive, I'm not asking you to ignore or accept these behaviors. In such cases, you need to seriously consider getting help or getting out of the relationship. At the same time, I can't stress enough that if you change to a healthier, nontoxic way of thinking, your partner will respond positively. Still, in the face of more extreme unreasonable or abusive behaviors, the future of the relationship needs to be evaluated. In such cases, consultation with a qualified mental health professional is helpful.

HOW TO PROVE YOUR TOXIC THOUGHTS WRONG

THE WAY TO develop healthy alternatives to your toxic thoughts is simple: *You need to gather evidence to dispute them.* Remember, toxic thoughts are simply distorted explanations for your partner's actions, statements, and behaviors. What most people don't realize is that challenging your toxic thoughts with sound, positive, alternative explanations based on evidence instead of emotion will make your relationship stronger and more rewarding.

You've probably heard the saying, "Put your money where your mouth is." When it comes to toxic thoughts like *He's constantly criticizing me,* I say put your money where your mouth is, with a twist. I ask you to prove that your partner is *not* always criticizing you.

Wait a minute! Shouldn't that be the other way around? Don't you need to prove that he *is* constantly criticizing you? No, and here's why: Once you're in the throes of toxic thinking, you're already going to be tuned in to evidence that supports your toxic claim, in this case that he's constantly critical (He told you last week that you talk too much and the week before he said you're always frowning). Instead, you need to gather evidence *against* your toxic thoughts by challenging your interpretation of your partner's words or actions. As you take this critical step, keep the following in mind:

Come Up with at Least Three Exceptions to the Behavior

Toxic thoughts tend to be all-encompassing so find exceptions to whatever types of toxic thoughts you are having. It is unlikely that your partner is always insensitive or a complete loser.

Kent felt that Jerome, his partner of several years, was "a complete bull in a china shop when it comes to emotional issues. He always says the worst possible thing. It's like he's trying to upset me on purpose." However, when Kent was encouraged to think of exceptions to this perception of Jerome, it wasn't that difficult: "Jerome was very attentive, sensitive, and understanding during my mother's death. He's also supportive when I'm having stress at work and he's been a constant source of strength since my father disowned me when I came out."

Kent couldn't help but admit that, in many ways, Jerome is a solid emotional partner. After all, it's hard to ignore the evidence. Kent was able to lose his anger toward Jerome. He was empowered to learn to ask his partner to be there for him, instead of getting stuck in a toxic thought quagmire of All or Nothing thinking and Label Slinging.

Like Kent, you will feel empowered in your relationship when you look for the exceptions to the toxic rule. One or two examples may convince you, but three or more are better. The more evidence you can get, the easier it will be to refute your toxic thoughts.

Pretend You're an Unbiased Third Party

Imagine that you've been hired as an outside, objective expert to testify in court and support your partner on points of conflict. By developing arguments in support of your partner's position, you become empathetic. As I discuss in greater detail later on, empathy is the ability to understand your partner's point of view. A deeper understanding of your partner's position on points of conflict will often help remove the roadblocks and their underlying toxic thoughts. This empathy-promoting exercise can be used by both of you to counter all types of toxic thoughts. Empathy—especially deep empathy—is the emotional glue that holds relationships together. It is also a very important way for couples to strengthen their relationships. To help you get into this mindset, imagine that you are being given $50,000 to find the evidence to defend your partner against your toxic accusations. (Wouldn't that be nice!)

Write It Down

It will help you to see your evidence in black and white. Magic changes can occur when you write down your positive thoughts on paper. Think about how good it feels when you've had positive things written about you. Do you remember the teachers who gave you good grades and those who made positive comments about your efforts and creativity? Didn't that feel good? (In contrast, remember how it hurt to see a poor grade or negative comments in red ink.) Writing down positive statements about your partner make you more mindful of the positive aspects of your relationship. Try it first on yourself—write down some specific positive things about you. They can be anything that matters to you, like the time you volunteered at your son's school or the appreciation you get from other parents for coaching your daughter's soccer team. Or your list may include how you're seen as a team player and a problem-solver at work. If doing this helps you feel good about yourself, why not give this gift to your partner? The more positive thoughts you write, the more you'll see your partner in a positive light.

REVISITING THE NINE TOXIC THOUGHT PATTERNS

LET'S REVISIT THE nine toxic thought patterns so you can see exactly how to create alternative thoughts for each one.

#1: Freeing Yourself from the All or Nothing Trap

In the last chapter, Sophie's All or Nothing thoughts led her to see her husband Jack as *always* inconsiderate for leaving folded laundry on top of the dryer and *constantly* leaving dirty dishes in the sink.

As Sophie took on the job of defending her husband against her toxic thought *He never thinks of my feelings*, we explored the various aspects of her relationship in which this was *not* the case. She told me that Jack encouraged and supported her to have four uninterrupted hours each week on the treadmill. During this time, he took full responsibility for the kids. Clearly, knowing how important exercise is to her, he was thinking of her feelings. As Sophie focused on Jack's support of her exercise time, she made a fascinating discovery; it wasn't the only evidence of her husband's support and generosity. When Sophie looked at her workout time as a generous offering from Jack, more examples of his considerateness and his other good qualities began to emerge. At first they trickled, but soon they poured into her mind. Clearly, it wasn't going to be too hard for Sophie to come up with at least three pieces of evidence to use against her toxic thoughts. I had Sophie write them down:

1. Jack is a caring father and often puts the kids to bed to give me a break.
2. He's a solid financial provider who is always generous with gifts.
3. He makes me laugh when I'm in a bad mood.
4. Jack makes me coffee in the morning even though he drinks tea.
5. Jack was incredibly supportive during my struggles with post-partum depression.
6. On occasion, he even puts the dishes away and folds the laundry.

The Better Alternative to Toxic Thinking 73

There, right in front of her, was the evidence Sophie needed to rid herself of her toxic thinking. Sophie was finally empowered to step back from her unrealistic toxic thoughts and see the reality: Jack is a good husband who frequently thinks of her feelings. And here's the best part—Sophie almost instantly lost her anger toward Jack. "After reviewing all of this evidence, how could I be mad at him?" Sophie told me. "In fact, I appreciate him even more. I feel like I should apologize for even having that toxic thought in the first place."

This kind of profound transformation is not unusual. You're probably tired of hearing this, but I'll say it again because it's so important: The key is to be aware that thoughts cause feelings, and that by changing your underlying thinking you can actually change how you feel.

Looking at the evidence and feeling more positively toward her husband helped Sophie focus on the big picture (all of Jack's considerate acts over a long period of time) and not on one inconsiderate act. When we feel threatened, we can lose sight of the big picture. The problem with toxic thinking is that it prevents us from looking at some very important parts of this picture—those parts that are more rational and positive. No partner or relationship is perfect, problems don't usually last forever, and two people, not one, play a role in problems.

Armed with her new positive thought that Jack *often thinks of my feelings*, Sophie is able to put a more realistic spin to her other thoughts. She is now able to calmly look at the evidence and Jack's actions in the proper perspective. When Jack piles dishes in the sink, Sophie tells herself, *Jack is not out to get me. He's been really busy this morning. He's cleaned out the garage and picked up the dry cleaning. He probably forgot that not putting the dishes away drives me crazy.*

Creating these alternative thoughts was a tremendous positive step for Sophie. By looking at the bigger picture (the whole morning and all of Jack's actions) instead of the little one (that one moment and the kitchen sink), Sophie is able to see Jack in a more reasonable and loving way.

Keep your language neutral. In keeping with the theme that your partner is who and what you *think* he or she is, consider the box below. As you can see, there are some words and phrases that are red flags for All or Nothing thoughts. If you replace these red-flag words with more reasonable and realistic words, you'll be better able to deal with All or Nothing thinking.

KEEP YOUR WORDS REASONABLE AND REALISTIC	
All or Nothing Toxic Words	Reasonable and Realistic Words
Always	Sometimes, at times
Never	Occasionally
All the time	In some cases
Nothing	Right now, some things
Everything	This one thing/ These couple of things

In fact, my clients tell me they are amazed at the dramatic, positive difference that just a few words can make. People quickly realize that once they break the habit of using their rigid All or Nothing words, their toxic thinking is practically eliminated.

MORE ALTERNATIVES TO ALL OR NOTHING TOXIC THINKING		
Toxic Thoughts	Evidence to the Contrary	Alternative Thoughts
"He never wants to talk about adoption."	"That's not true. Just the other day, he told me he was worried that a child brought up by a same-sex couple would be socially ostracized."	"This is a complicated and emotional issue. I need to be aware that just because he doesn't agree with me doesn't mean we're not communicating."
"She always has to be right."	"Hold on. Last week, she told me I made the right decision when the basement flooded."	"Sheri is often open-minded, but this issue seems really important to her."
"Nothing he does or says is fair."	"I'm doing it again! Steve is often fair about many things—like the housework and vacations."	"We agree on a lot of things. No couple agrees one hundred percent of the time."

But my partner really does always do this. You might be tempted to think that your situation is the exception. Naturally, many of my clients challenge me and say, "But he *really* always does this" or "She *really* never does that."

My response is to take them back to when they were first dating. I ask if the upsetting behavior also occurred at that time. More often than not, the behavior did not occur at that time, so it did not "always" occur. Even in the rare cases in which the behavior "always" occurred from day one, it certainly must not have mattered to the extent it does now, since the couple got together in the first place and are still together now.

The bottom line is that challenging toxic thoughts changes your perspective for the better. Because the MAP approach asks you to develop alternative explanations and gather evidence, you are naturally encouraged to see your partner's good qualities along with the negative ones. When you are able to step back and be more realistic, you are often able to be more accepting of your partner's annoying habits. You may decide, *It's not the biggest deal in the world,* and let it go.

But it really bugs me. You may decide to pursue the issue that's bothering you with your partner. That's fine, especially if you find that it is really bugging you. That's certainly preferable to leaving your issues unresolved or feeling angry or disappointed and not vocalizing your feelings. MAP is not about detoxifying your thinking so nothing will ever bother you again. That's not realistic. What MAP allows you to do is to connect with your partner about real issues in a way that is more supportive and fair. The combination of mindfulness, alternatives, and practice can all work together to take you, and your relationship, to a higher place. You will see your partner with more clarity, see issues in a less negative way, and problems will feel more manageable. The clearer perspective you get from MAP will allow you to effectively solve problems. As my uncle used to say to me, "You can't shake hands with a clenched fist."

In your more mindful state, you can stop yourself from expressing your toxic thoughts and instead express yourself in a more productive manner. As Suzanne told me, "Yes, I do feel that Ralph leaves the bathroom a mess quite a bit, but now I don't say, 'You're always a slob.' Instead I say, 'I would really appreciate it if you could help me keep the bathroom clean. It's a chore I can't stand.' And it works. More often than not, he will help me and we don't get in a big ridiculous fight about it. Becoming mindful helped me realize that he's not ignoring my feelings; he's just throwing towels on the floor."

In Chapter Nine, I'll discuss in more detail how to raise issues and fight fair with your partner. For now, let's continue to come up with better alternatives to your toxic thinking.

#2: Replacing Catastrophic Conclusions with Optimistic Opportunities

In Chapter Three, Claire was furious with Joel. Claire felt prey to Catastrophic Conclusions about how his part-time business venture would fail and result in the loss of their cars, house, and financial security.

Claire challenged her fear of bankruptcy by grounding herself in the facts:

- Joel has done a tremendous amount of research.
- Our accountant supported his new venture as a sound business opportunity.
- Joel has proven his business savvy in the past by making wise and careful investments.
- Many people ask for Joel's advice.
- The business broke even in the first year, which is unusual for new business ventures.

Claire was able to review the evidence and tell herself, *Joel is a smart guy. If anyone can make it work, he can. And if it doesn't work, we'll bounce back and be okay.*

Claire and Joel's story is a glowing example of how creating alternative thoughts can take you from Catastrophic Conclusions to Optimistic Opportunities.

MORE ALTERNATIVES TO CATASTROPHIC CONCLUSIONS		
Toxic Thoughts	Evidence to the Contrary	Alternative Thoughts
"Her babying of the boys will ruin their lives. They won't be able to fend for themselves."	"The boys are well-adjusted. They have many friends. They are able to stand up for themselves."	"I'm reacting out of fear that the boys will be sissies. This is ungrounded and unfair. Her female perspective will help them relate to women when they are older."
"She is never going to introduce me to her family. She's just stringing me along."	"I did meet her sister."	"Just because my family is open to my sexual orientation, that doesn't mean her whole family is."
"His mother is going to wreck our marriage."	"Nathan and I have a strong relationship. He usually defends me when I argue with his mother."	"His mother is a part of his life but so am I. Nathan is always patient with my mother. This isn't the end of the world."

#3: Exploding the *Should* Bomb Myth

When we met Dave and Diana, they were hurling a lot of *should*s at each other. Dave felt his wife Diana should get a better-paying job because she should know that he was stressed about money.

*Should*s and *ought*s can make you feel crazy because they actually may have some basis in reality. After all, Dave is allowed to want Diana to desire more money and Diana is allowed to want Dave to support her in her work choices.

As I explained to Dave, there's a big problem with *should*. By thinking in rigid, toxic *should*s, you put your partner at a disadvantage, by setting yourself up to believe that he or she is a bad, uncaring person if your demands are not met.

Think about it. At a very young age you learn to associate bad feelings with the word *should*. Every child has heard a parent saying that he or she should have done or should not have done something in particular, usually either stating or implying that the child is bad. We learn that when we do something that we *shouldn't* do, we are bad—and when we do not do things we *should* do, we are also bad. We learn this so well that we are able to elicit the same emotional response from ourselves about our partners when we use the word *should* as our parents did.

I've got some great news for you. Simply phrasing and reframing your alternative thoughts using the words *would like* instead of *should* can save you from The Three-D Effect in your relationship. *Should*s reflect our demanding, rigid, unrealistic expectations of our partners. *Should*s are immature and, like all toxic thoughts, can disrupt communication and erode intimacy over time. By saying *would like* instead of *should*, we relieve the pressure and rigidity of these expectations.

Should suggests *You must*, whereas *would like* suggests *Let's cooperate*. Enduring, satisfying relationships are based on cooperating, not mandating. Once Dave understood the baggage of the word *should*, he instantly knew the biggest piece of evidence against his toxic thought: He had never told Diana that he was worried about money. Just realizing that his wife couldn't read his mind and understand, enabled Dave to create this alternative: "I *would like* Diana to consider getting a better paying job or going on a tighter budget."

MORE ALTERNATIVES TO *SHOULD* BOMB TOXIC THOUGHTS		
Toxic Thoughts	**Evidence to the Contrary**	**Alternative Thoughts**
"Josh should know how I feel about this."	"It's unrealistic for me to assume he knows how I feel."	"I need to share how I feel so he can understand how important this is to me."
"He doesn't want me to meet his coworkers because he's ashamed of being gay."	"He did tell me that the managing partner doesn't like his employees to mix business with pleasure."	"I would like him to be less hung up on how the people in his conservative work environment perceive us as a gay couple. Yet I realize this does not mean he is less committed to me."
"She should be more excited for me."	"She's very preoccupied with her father's illness."	"I would like her to feel as enthusiastic as I do."

#4: Label Slinging Lassoed

Remember Jennifer and Scott? Jennifer toxically viewed Scott as a "couch potato" and Scott retaliated with the label "shopaholic."

Is Scott really a couch potato? Before you can gather evidence to dispute the label, you have to admit to what you're *really* saying. Calling someone a couch potato is not a compliment. The term connotes someone who is lazy, uninspired, and unambitious. I challenged Jennifer to look at the big picture and gather evidence against this label. Jennifer quickly came up with this evidence: Scott runs fifteen miles a week, works ten hours of overtime a week, and rises early to read the paper and help with chores. That's hardly the behavior of a lazy couch potato.

Label	What You're Really Saying
"You're a shopaholic."	"You spend too much money." "You're irresponsible with money." "You're obsessed with material items."
"You're a neat-freak."	"You're rigid." "You care more about cleaning than you do about me."
"You're stubborn."	"You don't listen to me." "You never consider my feelings."
"He's the crazy one."	"I find it impossible to understand him."
"You're lazy."	"I am so frustrated because I can't get you to do what I feel is important."
"You're insensitive."	"I wish you would pay attention to me."

Here's an interesting point about labeling. As Aaron Beck noted, the assigned labels are often the opposite of the partners' original perceptions about each other. In other words, the very qualities that often attract partners to each other come to be seen as negatives. The positive qualities of the labeled partner do not just evaporate. What happens over time is that stresses, disillusionment, and plain old familiarity lead to toxic thinking. When this happens, the negative aspects of your relationship become more prominent.

When they first met, Jennifer was attracted to Scott because he was "the easygoing one," the one who was able to sit back and relax. She'd felt that his ability to relax would stop her from being so serious all the time, from being such a go-getter. After a few years of marriage, however, Jennifer's positive label of Scott as "easygoing" became the negative label of "couch potato."

During my work with Jennifer, I helped her realize that she had a tendency to toxically label Scott because her married life was different from what she expected. Jennifer became more mindful that her desire for Scott to do home-improvement projects every weekend wasn't always fair. As her evidence showed, Scott worked several hours of overtime each week and needed some downtime. I helped Jennifer see that her negative perception of Scott was the polar opposite of her initial positive view of him.

I shared with Jennifer a chart of negative labels, which I use to help clients reframe their negative labels of their partners with more positive ones. Reframing the label you give your partner will encourage you to rethink your perceptions about him or her.

MORE ALTERNATIVES TO TOXIC LABELS	
Toxic Labels	Positive Reframing Labels
Stubborn	Determined
Selfish	Valuing himself
Jealous	Caring and protective
Unmotivated	Laid-back
Controlling	Confident
Passive	Accepting
Stingy	Cautious
Calculating	Deliberate
Anal	Careful
Pushy	Enthusiastic
Nuts or crazy	Unique

Interestingly, when I pressed Scott about his reasons for calling Jennifer a "shopaholic" (which really means "irresponsible with money"), he admitted that he really didn't think she had a problem with shopping or spending too much money. He was labeling her to "get back at her" for labeling him. "I felt like I had to make her seem not so perfect either," he said.

It is very common for one partner to retaliate against the other for Label Slinging. Changing your label for your partner from a toxic one to a more positive one will create magic in your relationship. As you begin to see your partner in a more understanding way, he or she will sense it and respond positively to you. *The less you negatively label, the more you and your partner become emotionally available to each other.*

#5: Ending Blame Game Pain

Walt and Gail were an example of how insidious and damaging toxic blame can be for couples. If you recall, this couple had been married for twenty-five years. Walt was beside himself with anger at Gail for her sexual shutdown that had lasted for seven years. He also blamed Gail for the couple's excessive credit card bills.

Gail, on the other hand, blamed Walt for being overly involved with his work, just like her father was when she was growing up. She blamed him for not being emotionally safe enough to discuss finances or any other issues. Each partner blamed the other; it was a mess.

It can be very seductive to believe that your relationship problems are the fault of your partner. After all, if you think it is entirely your partner's fault then that absolves you of any responsibility. But a relationship's problems are rarely the exclusive fault of one partner. It really does take two to make or break a relationship. While it might feel natural to blame your partner for your relationship problems, this strategy usually makes things worse.

Water seeks it's own level (and so do couples!). I'm going to tell you something that may surprise you, but I think you may need to hear it: *We are attracted to people at a similar mental health level to ourselves.*

Why is this such a big deal? Because often the partner who is blaming, the "blamer," perceives him- or herself as superior to the partner being blamed, the "blamee." Walt certainly fancied himself a saint for "putting up with" Gail. But since we are attracted to partners at our own mental health level, neither partner is above the other. Each person has shared responsibility for choosing to be in the relationship and for what they get out of the relationship.

I have said all along that it is best to focus on the only party in a conflict you have any control over—yourself—and to teach yourself how to think and react differently when facing relationship conflicts. While it's common to blame the other partner for conflict in relationships, this strategy will not resolve the conflicts. Remember, when you take responsibility and make changes, more often than not your partner will respond positively.

MORE ALTERNATIVES TO BLAME GAME TOXIC THOUGHTS		
Toxic Thoughts	Evidence to the Contrary	Alternative Thoughts
"She made me give up my dream to become an engineer."	"I could have pursued my education at night."	"I made sacrifices and decisions and I need to be held accountable."
"He's ruined our chances of having new friends."	"I was the one who shot down the idea of going to our church social."	"Friendships can't be just his decision. I have just as much responsibility to reach out."
"Her fear of change kept us in this house."	"She was the one who gave me the idea to go back to school."	"Sure, I wish we could move to a bigger home sooner, but I can't blame her. In fact, in the long run, I'll thank her for saving more money."

In the case of toxic Blame Gaming, your evidence really consists of you admitting that you have contributed to the problem. This is about taking responsibility and being a grown-up. Walt was able to see that while Gail had lost interest in sex, he had not tried to rekindle it by really listening to her, planning romantic getaways, and paying greater attention to foreplay; all the things Gail had told him she needed to feel sexually aroused. Walt also admitted that he yelled at Gail whenever she tried to discuss finances with him. Of course she wasn't going to check in with him before making credit card purchases.

For her part, Gail was able to see that she shut down sexually with Walt in an attempt to protect herself from his lack of emotional availability. This was also Gail's way to punish Walt. Keep in mind that neither party woke up each morning planning to hurt the other with blame. But their lack of mindfulness that they were even stuck in the Blame Game had them doing the same dance over and over, and caused considerable damage to their relationship. Again, as another vicious cycle of toxic thinking, the Blame Game can become relentless.

#6: Rewiring Emotional Short-Circuits

You may recall the story of Stacy and Kevin. Stacy's father had left the family when she was young. This left Stacy prone to feeling abandoned in relationships. After having been estranged from her father for so many years, Stacy was recently informed by one of her siblings that her father had a terminal illness. Stacy had mixed thoughts and feelings about this. Kevin started to become frustrated because he wanted to be supportive but felt increasingly attacked and ignored by Stacy. One night, Kevin erupted, screaming that he was sick of Stacy's moods.

Emotional Short-Circuiting can cause serious intimacy problems. Like other toxic thoughts, Emotional Short-Circuiting is laden with distortions, usually about the other person's emotional stability. Partners who Emotionally Short-Circuit can become very judgmental, thinking *There's something wrong with him*, or *She's just nuts*.

The ability to feel vulnerable disappears when Emotional Short-Circuiting occurs. Ironically, when Kevin Emotionally Short-Circuited he became unavailable to Stacy, which only exacerbated her feelings of abandonment. As was the case for Kevin, the key word for those who Emotionally Short-Circuit is *can't*. In one form or another the thought is *I can't handle him (her)* or *I can't take it*. Typically, this occurs with a partner who has great difficulty relating to the emotionality of the other partner. I helped Kevin to explore this negative mindset and how it limited him with Stacy. Kevin learned to focus on all the times that Stacy had eventually returned to a more level state of mind after she calmed down. He used this evidence to rewire his own emotional responses to Stacy. He learned not to use logic (or a timer) on her feelings but rather to just accept her feelings without judging them. This sense of increased acceptance and patience from Kevin, in turn, empowered Stacy to reconnect with her father and make amends with him shortly before he died. Needless to say, this mutual understanding brought Kevin and Stacy closer than they had ever been before.

If you Emotionally Short-Circuit, you need to become mindful of your *can't*s. A useful alternative is *will try* or a similar thought that will help you handle your partner's emotions. Partners prone to Emotional Short-Circuiting often genuinely want to help their partners but become frustrated when they feel helpless themselves. Sadly, one partner who Emotionally Short-Circuits can unknowingly leave the other partner feeling devalued.

Here are some ways to use alternatives to avoid Emotionally Short-Circuiting. Use these types of alternatives and your relationship will become more stable.

MORE ALTERNATIVES TO EMOTIONAL SHORT-CIRCUIT		
Toxic Thoughts	Evidence to the Contrary	Alternative Thoughts
"I can't handle her mood swings."	"Actually, I don't usually find it so difficult to support her."	"Part of the appeal in her is that she is sensitive about things. I have to remind myself how rewarding her sensitivity is to me."
"He's driving me away."	"We've had many months of good communication."	"I find it difficult to handle his jealousy. I'm optimistic that this can get better. How can we work through this?"
"She's too much."	"I can be pretty demanding in my own way."	"Her intensity can really turn me on. It's okay if it overwhelms me at times because I can remind myself that we will soon move past it."

The occasional Emotional Short-Circuit can be dealt with effectively by using the alternative thinking strategies I have shown above.

However, if one partner (or both) has emotional reactions that are overly excessive or obsessive, like washing hands one hundred times or crying for several days, professional help needs to be considered. Emotional volatility like this can signal depression, anxiety, or another mental health issues that may warrant professional attention.

7: Taming Your Overactive Imagination with Truth

Evidence is truly critical for overcoming this toxic thought pattern!

Revisit the story of Lisa and Jerry. Lisa, Jerry's wife of seven years, came home late from a work-related Christmas party. Jerry's Overactive Imagination, fueled by his deep-seated belief that he is not an adequate provider, led him to conclude that Lisa was having an affair with a "rich doctor." Sadly for Jerry, he did not voice his concerns to Lisa. He did not ask Lisa why she was late or talk with her about the party. He stewed and worried in silence.

Overactive Imagination results from a need for control. Remember, the more out of control one partner believes the other partner to be, the more in control he or she tries to be—often by using faulty, distorted, or accusatory explanations to fill in the blanks.

When one partner's expectations for a certain type of response from the other partner are not met, toxic thoughts involving the Overactive Imagination are easily triggered. Partners then harmfully (and unknowingly) rely on their anxiety to give them answers. (Again, this is similar to what occurs in Catastrophic Conclusions but with Catastrophic Conclusions one partner exaggerates the consequences of actual events and with Overactive Imagination, thoughts are not based in reality at all.)

Because of the anxiety underlying Overactive Imagination, the breathing and mantra advice in Chapter Four can be particularly helpful in conquering this toxic thought pattern.

The best way to counter Overactive Imagination is to get evidence based in reality. Reality is the antidote to anxious, irrational thoughts. Anxiety is laden with a fear of the unknown, such as *This will never end. I just don't see a solution in sight,* and *I'm scared this will never get better.* It makes good sense, then, that gathering "knowns" is the best strategy to beat anxiety. You often will be able to do this on your own by repeatedly reminding yourself of the facts. Jerry overcame his anxiety with these thoughts:

- Lisa has never given me any real reason to think her commitment to our relationship has changed.
- She once swore to me that if she was ever unhappy or dissatisfied with me in our relationship that she would be honest with me.
- Lisa has proven time and time again that money is not her number-one priority. She is very happy living in this neighborhood and recently commented that she hoped neither of us get transferred so we can stay here.

Your anxiety level, however, may have escalated to the point where you're not able to counter these toxic thoughts on your own. You may have to check in with your partner. But your partner may be encouraged to Emotionally Short-Circuit on you, especially if this issue has caused tension between you before. Your partner may think, *Your suspicions are too much! I can't have a relationship without trust.*

Honesty is usually the best policy. My advice is to detoxify the thought as much as you can on your own and then admit it to your partner, but not in an accusatory fashion. If you can approach the subject in a positive and honest way, you have a much better chance of getting a positive response from your partner.

Jerry was able to say to Lisa, "I know that you love me and that we have a good relationship. I'm feeling a little anxious right now and I'm willing to own that this is my stuff. Sometimes I get insecure and my head fills with thoughts about you not being committed to me. I'm asking if you can just hear me without attaching judgment and accept that I am working on it. Is it okay to ask you for some reassurance to help me with this?"

Anxiety can play a big role in Overactive Imagination. If you find yourself obsessing to the point where it is dominating your life (you can't focus on anything else, you can't sleep), consult a trained mental health professional. And keep this in mind. Even if your worst fears come true, your life will not be over. Life goes on and so will you.

MORE ALTERNATIVES TO OVERACTIVE IMAGINATION		
Toxic Thoughts	Evidence to the Contrary	Alternative Thoughts
"We're going to break up."	"She just told me how much she values our relationship."	"Just because she's busy and has other things on her mind, that doesn't mean she doesn't love me."
"He's been talking about work stresses a lot lately. He's going to get laid off."	"His company's profits were up by ten percent last quarter and his department exceeded its budget. He also won salesperson of the quarter."	"He probably just needs to vent."
"She doesn't want to have sex. She must find me unattractive."	"We made love two days ago and it was wonderful."	"I need to stop thinking this way. She's most likely tired from her long day."

8: Betting On Reality to End the Head Game Gamble

Let's take another look at Allen and Linda's story. They lived together for eight years and were Head Game Gamblers. Allen thought Linda had a hidden agenda when she was affectionate and kind to him. He thought, *Here she goes again. I know how she operates. She wants to visit her sister for the weekend, so she is just turning on the charm now.* Allen erroneously interpreted Linda's kindness as evidence that she was manipulating him. He lost sight of the behavior at hand because he assumed that she had ulterior motives.

With this toxic thought pattern, the Head Game Gamble, partners think they can read each other's minds. Ironically, years of togetherness and shared experience can make the Head Game Gamble even more likely. That's because partners often believe that spending years together automatically means knowing how the other feels. The Head Game Gamble can also manifest when one partner erroneously believes the other partner's specific behaviors or actions are directed at him or her. Your partner thinks, *She woke up early and cleaned the kitchen to "tell me" that I don't do enough* or your partner coming home slightly delayed from a meeting is interpreted as, *He's obviously paying me back because I didn't clean up the garage like I said I would.*

So, the Head Game Gambler may think, *She's paying me back for watching football all afternoon by not making dinner* when in fact the partner feels like she's coming down with the flu and needs to rest. Or *He only said that my new haircut isn't attractive because I said he's going bald* when in fact your new hairstyle isn't as flattering as the old one. When you make assumptions about your partner's behavior you will often be incorrect. I always remember the amusing saying about the word "assume." When you assume, you make an "ass" of "u" and "me."

MORE ALTERNATIVES TO HEAD GAME GAMBLE		
Toxic Thoughts	Evidence to the Contrary	Alternative Thoughts
"She got me golf balls so I'll have to let her host her book club here."	"She always buys my golf balls when they're on sale."	"She indulges my hobbies, I should indulge hers."
"She was only nice to my mother because she wants me to accept her new friends, who I don't like."	"She has been unconditionally nice to my mother many times before."	"I know she has tried a number of times to make an effort to connect with my mother. I'm just going to accept her actions without judging them."
"This sudden attentiveness must be a setup."	"He often gives me consideration without strings attached."	"He is trying to reach out and be kind. I'm going to work on accepting this behavior at face value."

If your partner is truly exhibiting unacceptable behaviors such as repeatedly being passive-aggressive, you need to calmly but firmly address this. You need to say, "This isn't acceptable anymore." There is a difference between developing alternative explanations for your own Head Game Gambles and your partner actually behaving in a passive-aggressive manner (such as deliberately leaving dishes in the sink, making noise while you are trying to sleep, or intentionally and inconsiderately interrupting with "important questions" as you study for your night-school exam). In such cases you need to assert yourself and let your partner know that you will not accept such treatment (see Chapter Nine for more advice on fighting fair). If such toxic behaviors continue, you should consider getting outside help or urging your partner to see a therapist or counselor.

9: Relishing Reality Instead of Disillusionment Doom

If you recall from Chapter Three, Terri wished that she and John could go back to the days when life was simpler and they had far fewer material possessions. Things seemed real and uncomplicated in those days. Now, Terri feels like John has sold out to corporate greed and has grown materialistic. All the money they have feels meaningless.

It's not unusual for partners to feel betrayed, disappointed, or let down when those rose-colored glasses begin to fog up and crack under the stress of real life. Couples often begin to argue about spending, bathroom habits, or personality traits, which obstructs their ability to work out their real issues. When I first mentioned Disillusionment Doom in Chapter Three, I said that some people are inclined to get bored easily and crave new things. If this is the case for you, you will likely be asking too much if you want your partner (or any partner) to be a new and exciting person every few months or years.

Breaking out of Disillusionment Doom means looking for new ways to think about, and do things with, your partner.

Individuals who tend to be intense or perfectionistic are particularly at risk for Disillusionment Doom. Perfectionists are usually demanding not only of themselves, but also of the ones they love. Often their justification is *I'm no harder on you than I am on myself.* That way of thinking is a setup for emotional hurts in intimate relationships. The feelings of vulnerability that come with being in an intimate relationship can trigger you to be defensive in the face of inevitable misunderstandings. When you are feeling defensive, you may then find yourself more accepting and forgiving toward *yourself* instead of your partner. For this reason, you may indeed be harder on your partner than on yourself. If you have this type of personality, it is particularly important for you to monitor your thinking for Disillusionment Doom.

It's also important to make sure you're not just using Disillusionment Doom to cover up a deeper emotional issue that you're uncomfortable handling. This was a problem for Janis and Katie, a long-term couple. Janis was upset with Katie for volunteering much of her time at a local hospital. "Never during the earlier days of our relationship would Katie have been so willing to give up precious time we could have together," she said.

As we worked together, it became clear that perhaps Janis was not disillusioned with Katie's way of choosing to spend her time so much as she was disappointed with herself. Janis was between jobs and her life felt meaningless because she had never found satisfying work. Instead of facing this uncomfortable fact, it was more comfortable to find fault with the person closest to her—Katie.

Fortunately, Janis was open to seeing her lack of job fulfillment as the source of her disillusionment. Janis and I did some career interest assessment, and eventually she went back to school to become a chef. When she began working again, her night hours conveniently overlapped with Katie's volunteering commitments. Not surprisingly, the couple worked together to find time for each other, even in the face of their hectic schedules. Each partner became more fulfilled as an individual and the relationship improved dramatically.

This tendency to "misplace" your feelings onto your partner happens quite a bit. You don't like something in yourself, so you "project" it, or assign it to the other person. Once you detoxify your thinking, you will be in a better position to discover your real issue.

MORE ALTERNATIVES TO DISILLUSIONMENT DOOM		
Toxic Thoughts	**Evidence to the Contrary**	**Alternative Thoughts**
"She watched her weight when I married her."	"It's hard for most women to keep their figure after childbirth."	"I've gained weight myself. Nobody is perfect. Maybe we can find some ways to work on our health together."
"I wish he was patient like he used to be."	"He's under a lot of stress." "He was patient with me when I was a basketcase after my mom died."	"I need to keep that in mind so I can be more understanding of what he is going through."
"He doesn't want to go out and have fun anymore."	"He seems tired tonight. He did rake the whole yard."	"It's difficult to be spontaneous now; maybe I should try planning a night out when we'll both be ready and rested."

TO SUM IT ALL UP

REMEMBER EPICTETUS, WHO said, "Man is not disturbed by events alone but by his perception of events." This is a huge yet extremely underappreciated truth about the human condition. The freedom to choose our thoughts has been the subject of many great philosophers. Buddha, for example, said, "What we think, we become." But so few of us take advantage of this universal, time-tested truth.

Now you are empowered to gather evidence to dispute and counter your toxic thinking and to develop better, healthier alternatives.

Some people ask me, "How long do I have to do this work?" It's true that gathering your evidence and developing alternatives is work, but it's far less work than dividing up all your possessions, posting your profile on a singles' Web site, or working out custody arrangements.

You won't have to do this work so diligently forever. Just as your toxic thoughts were once automatic, your better way of thinking will become automatic, too. Soon you will be able to dispute your toxic thoughts in an instant. It just takes a some time, practice, and patience.

6 Practice Makes Not Perfect, but Much Better

NOW YOU REALIZE the importance of mindfulness when it comes to your toxic thoughts, and how to use alternative thoughts to displace them. Putting this together, you've got an easy, no-nonsense way to zap your toxic thoughts. Now let's move on to the last part of MAP and further empower you to practice these skills in your life.

WHAT EXACTLY DOES PRACTICE MEAN FOR YOU?

YOU KNOW HOW to practice a tennis serve or knitting, but how do you practice having a better relationship?

Practice in your relationship encompasses three important steps:

1. Implementing positive thoughts and actions *over time*.
2. Making a commitment to remember to be mindful that every relationship needs work and commitment.
3. Keeping yourself mindful of your toxic thoughts and challenging them with alternatives.

I wish I could say that you will never have to practice these skills, but that would not be true. We live in a society that provides quite a few fantasies about how romance should be—easy and carefree—and some people become disappointed when they learn that they have to work at keeping their relationship vibrant and meaningful.

But we all have to work to get, and keep, the things that we want in life. If you want a healthier, more fulfilling relationship, you have to work at it, at least from time to time. As my father used to tell me, "If you want to dance, you have to pay the fiddler."

Maybe that's corny, but it's true. Practice means working on your relationship during the good and not so good times. Practice means accepting that your relationship satisfaction is a journey rather than a destination. Practice is staying committed to finding the good in your partner even when he or she disappoints or upsets you.

Every successful athlete knows what it means to "put in the work." The same goes for accomplished musicians, entertainers, and other professionals. Famous high-achievers may have been born with God-given talent, but they had to shape it and hone it. The same goes for relationships; even the great ones require work.

"WHY DO I HAVE TO DO ALL THE WORK?"

I DON'T JUST counsel couples. I counsel individuals who can't get their partners to come to counseling. I hear frustrated people say, "Yes, but why *should* I have to do *all* the work? Why am *I* the one who has to give in to make this relationship better?"

My response is, "Don't go down that road."

Let me offer you the wisdom of Stephen Covey, author of *The Seven Habits of Highly Effective People*, to support my point. He talks about the idea of "inside out versus outside in." Covey means that you should not worry about waiting for others to change for you, but instead make the changes for yourself. He also means that you should do for others instead of waiting for them to do for you. It is very likely that your partner will respond positively to your own work. Give it some time.

Operating with the *What's in it for me?* mindset sets you up for more toxic thinking and some big headaches. It tricks you into thinking that your partner doesn't do anything for you or the good of the relationship. You may toxically label him or her as uncaring, unloving, unaffectionate, boring, thoughtless, or inattentive. You may see yourself as the one doing everything for the good of the relationship. But when you take this attitude, you fail to see how you influence (but do not cause) your partner's behavior. (Each individual is responsible for his or her own behavior.) Specifically, you fail to see how your own toxic thinking influences your partner's behavior. You fail to see how it takes two to make a relationship and two to break it.

Relationships have a very difficult time surviving and thriving when the partners are immature, self-centered, and only see how they are affected. Remember, being mindful means being aware that all your thoughts and behaviors impact and affect your relationship—for better and worse.

Now let me also say that you did not get into your relationship to be treated poorly, ignored, or abandoned. Being abused or denigrated, managing the demands of the housework alone, being subjected to repeated reckless spending, raising the kids without support, being deprived of a sex life, or putting up with problematic or immature behavior is not what I am asking of you. If this is occurring in your relationship, your partner needs to make some major changes. Individual counseling may be helpful and you both will likely need couple's counseling. If your partner will not cooperate with counseling, you need to face the fact that your partner will probably never change. Then you have to decide to either try living with him or her the best you can or move on to a new and hopefully more satisfying relationship. I am all for trying to save relationships, but in the face of repeated hurts and insensitivity from your partner, it may be best to move on. Such decisions are usually very difficult.

WHY DO YOU need to be patient while making the transition from toxic to healthy thinking? Shouldn't these techniques work right away? Many of my clients do report that by countering and reframing their toxic thoughts into more healthy alternatives, they start to feel instantly closer to their partners. Still, why do many others need time, sometimes several weeks or even four to six months before the benefits of detoxifying the relationship are fully realized?

Because it takes time to toxify and it takes time to detoxify. Over time, you form perceptions of your partner. When you think toxically over time, all it takes is the very presence of your partner to trigger such thoughts (*Here she is, Miss Selfish* or *Great, here comes the man who never thinks about anyone but himself*). To undo these associations you must be mindful of countering them. I've shown you how to use alternatives; now it is up to you to follow through. Remember, being mindful means remembering the big picture— that relationships have easy and not so easy times and that they require ongoing maintenance.

When the toxic thoughts diminish and your relationship improves, you (and your partner) are still prone to falling back into the old feelings of anger, hurt, fear, rejection, or anxiety. Old habits die slow, sometimes very slow, deaths. It is very important to try to pinpoint which of the nine toxic thought patterns are influencing your feelings. And trust me, if you look close enough, you'll quickly realize how challenging and disputing your toxic thoughts with alternatives has helped to bring about improvement in your relationship. Now let's move on to the activities you can use to practice your toxic thought–busting skills on your own. Later on, I'll introduce you to some activities you can do with your partner to enhance your communication skills and intimacy. But for now you need to work on detoxifying your thoughts. Do these practice exercises on a regular basis for a month or so and I promise you'll be amazed at the results.

Activity #1: Breathing Your Way to Mindfulness

You know that keeping a cool head is very important in learning to be mindful and to control toxic thinking. But sometimes you will need more than a few deep breaths. (Even if you're calm, this exercise can take you to a deeper, even more meaningful state of relaxation.)

The following exercise is designed to help you return to mindfulness through breath and visualization. You can even do this while driving (just don't close your eyes!).

1. Close your eyes (if you're able).
2. Breathe in through your nose to a count of four.
3. Visualize (imagine) your breath as it goes down your windpipe, and into your diaphragm. Feel your stomach and then your chest expand as you breathe in. Allow your entire body to expand with the breath.
4. Now slowly breathe out through your mouth to a count of seven. Completely empty your lungs of air.
5. Visualize all your stress and tension leaving your body as you breathe out.
6. Repeat four times.
7. Now relax and reflect on what it actually feels like to calm yourself down. Think about how calming yourself in this way will enable you to manage your toxic thinking, improve your relationship, and find greater harmony in your life.
8. Use visualizations to further calm youself. One of my clients likes to visualize a fireman putting out her toxic thoughts like a fire. Another, who teaches kickboxing, likes to visualize that he's punching his toxic thoughts away. Still another imagines her body being filled with healing blue energy as she inhales and toxic red energy leaving her body as she exhales. You can try any of these suggestions or come up with a visualization of your own, like walking on the beach.
9. If you can, or choose to, write down how calming yourself will help you manage your toxic thinking, which in turn will help you improve your relationship.

Practice Makes Not Perfect, but Much Better

Practice this exercise as often as you can. I try to do this at least two times a day. Even when I'm not full of toxic thoughts, I just like the way it relaxes me.

Activity #2: Get To Know Your Toxic Thoughts

Mindfulness of your toxic thoughts takes work and discipline. The rewards of being able to control your toxic thoughts are nothing short of amazing. To help you become skilled at detoxifying your thinking, you need to understand how you think on a deeper level. I've devised a simple three-step exercise to help you do this.

Step One: Review the Nine Toxic Thought Patterns

Feel free to take a few minutes to review Chapter Three for more detail.

#1: The All or Nothing Trap: You see your partner as negatively either always or never doing things.

#2: Catastrophic Conclusions: One partner exaggerates negative actions and events concerning the other partner.

#3: The *Should* Bomb: One partner assumes the other will meet one or more of his or her needs—just because he or she should know about these needs.

#4: Label Slinging: You unfairly negatively label your partner and lose sight of his or her positive qualities.

#5: The Blame Game: You unfairly and irrationally blame your partner for relationship issues.

#6: Emotional Short-Circuit: One partner convinces him- or herself that his or her partner's emotions can't be "handled."

#7: Overactive Imagination: You reach negative conclusions about your partner that are not based in reality.

#8: Head Game Gamble: You try to outsmart your partner by erroneously assuming he or she has certain motives.

#9: Disillusionment Doom: Partners focus on idealized expectations of their partner that are rooted in the past.

Step Two: Answer Eight Questions for Mindful Self-Reflection

1. To which of the nine toxic thought patterns are you most prone?
3. Looking back honestly, in which relationship(s) have you had these toxic thoughts?
4. What damage do these toxic thoughts do to yourself?
5. What damage do these toxic thoughts do to your partner?
6. What damage do these toxic thoughts do to your relationship?
7. Is there evidence that can help you challenge these toxic thoughts?
8. What alternatives to these toxic thoughts can you generate?
9. What benefits would detoxifying your thoughts offer in your relationship?

Step Three: Share Your Answers with Your Partner (Optional)

You certainly don't have to share your answers with your partner, but I think it can help. Sharing your toxic thoughts with your partner from time to time can be very illuminating to both of you and can bring you closer together. Not only can you better understand yourself, your partner can better understand you. One caution to keep in mind: When preparing to share toxic thoughts with your partner, you must proceed with sensitivity. Stress how much you desire to get closer as a couple. Explain how coming up with alternatives for your toxic thoughts is important for your own emotional health. Stress the positive qualities about your partner first. Be very specific and ask for the "green light" from your partner to discuss your toxic thoughts. Don't say, "You're a good guy, but I get really upset with you and here's why." Rather, say something like, "I value how many hours you put in at work and how you help out with the kids. I also appreciate how gentle and kind you are with me. Yet it bothers me that I still find myself losing track of what you really do because I get focused on thinking that you 'should' know when I need space. Sometimes I feel smothered, but a lot of this is my stuff. I'd like to share with you some of what goes on in my head so that you can better understand what makes me tick, and what I'm working on so that I can think in healthier ways. Are you okay with me talking to you about this?"

Jasmine, for example, found that sharing her answers to the above questions with her fiancé Randy allowed her to get past a huge toxic thinking hurdle. She had found herself stuck in the All or Nothing Trap and doing some serious Label Slinging: *I can never give him enough. He's just a needy sponge that wants to suck me dry.*

When Jasmine did this exercise with Randy, she was deeply encouraged with the positive results. She told me about this during her next session. "I was totally surprised, pleasantly surprised. Randy was incredible. He started to get defensive but I made it clear that I was not putting him on trial. Then he really thanked me for being honest with him. He said that he could sometimes sense some tension from me when he was affectionate. He was silently frustrated and having some of his own toxic thoughts. He was saying to himself, 'She never appreciates anything I do.' When I shared my toxic thoughts, he told me his and we came away from the conversation feeling excited because I don't think a lot of couples really share on this level."

Some of my clients prefer to do this exercise on their own and keep the answers private. Do what works best for you. Certainly the goal here is not to constantly tell your partner about every thought going through your head. I don't advocate you phoning your partner while he or she is in the middle of a meeting and saying, "Honey, I want to tell you that I'm having toxic thoughts about you right now, but I think I'm working through them! It's okay, I just wanted to let you know, but you can go back to work."

Again, be sensitive to your partner and he or she will be much more likely to accept what you're saying.

Activity #3: Be Mindful of Your Partner's Good Qualities

It's important to maintain mindfulness of your partner's good qualities, especially when you're convinced (thanks to toxic thinking) that he or she has too few. Focusing on the good helps you keep that important "big picture" in perspective. Remaining aware of his or her strong points helps you to stay mindful of the value of your relationship, and your partner's worth, to develop healthy alternatives to toxic thoughts. The following exercise takes five to ten minutes; it will help you keep the big picture of your relationship in focus:

Make a list of your partner's strengths and weaknesses. Every day for fourteen days, add a new positive quality to your partner's list of virtues. Share each virtue with him or her. What a gift this is! Doing this demonstrates to your partner that you are paying attention and enjoying the qualities that are uniquely his or hers. At the same time, you are training yourself to enjoy what your partner already is and not longing for what he or she has yet to become. Remember that mindfulness is wanting and appreciating what you already have.

As a guide for this exercise, ask yourself, "Out of all these fine qualities of my partner, which one do I value the most?" Make sure that you appreciate this quality each day. How would your life be different if your partner lacked this quality?

Commit five to ten minutes a day over the next two weeks to writing down your partner's good qualities. There is nothing like the magic of putting pencil to paper. It really works. You can even use your evidence-gathering from the last chapter to get started. Remember how Sophie was able to rethink her toxic thought about Jack—*He never thinks of my feelings.* As she started to list the evidence for why this wasn't true, Jack's good qualities emerged. Completing the first part of this exercise was a snap for Sophie:

Evidence	Good Quality/Qualities
Jack is a caring father and often puts the kids to bed to give me a break.	Good Dad. Helpful with kids.
He's a solid financial provider who is always generous with gifts.	Good provider. Generous.
He makes me laugh when I'm in a bad mood.	Good sense of humor.
Jack makes me coffee in the morning even though he drinks tea.	Thoughtful and caring.

Activity #4: Give Yourself a Reality Check with Twelve Anti-Toxidants

In your continued quest to stay mindful, refer to this list of "anti-toxidants." The opposite of toxic thoughts, these are positive coping statements to help you combat your irrational, toxic thinking toward your partner. Consider mindfulness as having the awareness to realize that you can call upon anti-toxidants such as these. You take action by thinking them, believing them, and experiencing the resulting positive emotional health and harmony you feel by using them to dispute your toxic thoughts.

Some of my clients tell me they write the anti-toxidants down in journals or on index cards. Jason, for example, was really having a hard time shedding his toxic thoughts. "My parents were very negative people," he told me. "In our house, not only was the glass half empty, it had a chip in it. For me, breaking out of toxic thoughts, both directed at myself and at Lydia [his longtime girlfriend] was a struggle. I actually wrote the anti-toxidants down on index cards and left them all over the house and in my desk at work. I needed to see them all the time for the first month after we started counseling. Gradually, it gets easier. But I do still like to read them once in a while."

Put the anti-toxidants to work, use them to arrest your toxic thoughts, and see how you immediately start to feel closer to your partner.

The Twelve Relationship Anti-Toxidants
1. Even Mother Teresa would not have embraced my toxic thoughts.
2. I am individually responsible for my thoughts and feelings toward myself and toward my partner.
3. I am not perfect, nor is my partner.
4. My relationship can be satisfying even if my partner doesn't meet all my needs.
5. My off-the-charts, inflamed, angry thoughts toward my partner suggest that I am thinking about him or her in a toxic, irrational manner.

6. Countering my toxic thoughts leaves me feeling more objective and gives me more opportunities to work out conflicts with my partner.

7. The toxic thoughts I am thinking right now can influence me to appear less attractive to my partner.

8. When my needs and desires are not met, I will feel some sadness, anger, and disappointment. This is normal. Everybody goes through this.

9. When my rigid demands (driven by my toxic thoughts) are not met, I will feel unhealthy negative emotions such as rage, shock, horror, deep depression, or panic.

10. Strengthening my own ability to dispute my toxic thoughts will help my partner to be less of a toxic thinker.

11. When my partner makes mistakes I will forgive him (her) because he (she) is only human.

12. I can still feel good about my relationship, even if I don't feel thrilled about certain aspects of it — and my partner has the same right.

Activity #5: Practice Ten Commandments for Detoxification

In *How To Make Yourself Happy and Remarkably Less Disturbable*, Albert Ellis gives readers helpful strategies for challenging negative beliefs directed toward themselves. Extrapolating from Ellis's work and adding my own strategies, I compiled a list of ten commandments for a balanced, nontoxic relationship. Like the anti-toxidants, many of my clients review this list each day and find it very empowering to their relationships.

Tell yourself, I will make a commitment to:

1. remember how I felt empowered by realizing how much my relationship problems came from my own toxic thinking.

2. keep a list of the twelve anti-toxidants handy and review them daily or as needed to keep fresh in my mind.

3. realize the difference between my right to have normal negative feelings about _____ (your intimate partner) when

misunderstandings and miscommunications occur, and the mistake of bringing on relationship-crippling toxic thoughts.

4. remind myself how toxic thinking about myself can lead to depression, anxiety, and anger problems. I will keep this as proof that it similarly can damage my relationship.

5. be vigilant for my body's signals like shallow breathing and sweaty hands (see Chapter Four), warning me about my toxic thoughts.

6. assume that my partner has good intentions. He (she) doesn't want to hurt me on purpose.

7. own up to my immature behaviors directed at my partner, including the silent treatment, insulting him (her), abusing alcohol or drugs, or cheating on him (her).

8. stay mindful of all the things my partner does that I appreciate.

9. continue to dispute my toxic thoughts using evidence.

10. generate alternative explanations for my partner's undesirable behaviors.

Activity #6: Use "I" Instead of "You" Statements

As you will see, beginning your thoughts and statements with "I" instead of "you" will be helpful as well. *You* thoughts (*You're making a mountain out a mole hill again*) are more likely to incite negative feelings than *I* thoughts (*I don't understand why you're so upset*). That is because "You" statements tell the listener that he or she is "wrong" and you are "right." "You" statements feel accusatory.

Keep in mind that, as with any toxic thought, some if not all of these thoughts become spoken words. The benefit of changing your thoughts is that it will also help you change your words. So instead of saying, "You're such a know-it-all," you can say, "I understand that you think you're right, but I see it a different way."

If you are recovering from Blame Game or Label Slinging toxic thought patterns, it's especially important to be mindful of using "I" versus "You" statements. These two toxic thoughts easily lend themselves to hurling accusatory statements, like "You ruined our vacation," and "You're such a basket case."

Stan and Margaret couldn't believe what an incredible difference changing just one word could make in their ability to communicate and solve problems.

Stan: "Until I started paying attention to how I addressed Margaret, I had no idea how often I was saying things like, 'But you did . . .' Very accusatory. No wonder she used to refuse to talk to me sometimes!"

Margaret: "Focusing on saying 'I' forces you to pay attention to how you're speaking to your partner. It helped me choose my words more carefully. I know that it helped me avoid pitfalls in my communication with Stan."

Here are some more examples to show you the transforming power of *one little word*:

"You" Statements	"I" Statements
"You never let me finish." (All or Nothing)	"I would like to finish making my point."
"You think I'm just sitting here goofing off." (Overactive Imagination)	"I wish I could make you understand how hard I'm working and how frustrated I feel."
"You were the one who wanted the blue paint." (Blame Game)	"I wasn't crazy about the blue paint."
"You get too upset." (Emotional Short-Circuit)	"I wish I could understand why this affects you so deeply."
"You are going to make the house more and more cluttered until we won't ever be able to get it cleaned up." (Catastrophic Conclusion)	"I would like to explore how we can work together to keep ahead of the house demands."

Activity #7: Actions Speak Louder than Words:
Twelve Positive Relationship Resolutions

In addition to staying mindful, practice also means putting positive behaviors into action and avoiding negative behaviors. I'll never forget Charlie, who had complained that his girlfriend was "a bitch." He said this in front of her. No wonder she was thinking of leaving him. As I probed about the nature of his relationship, he acknowledged calling her obscene names, holding grudges, nagging, and throwing past hurts in her face. Charlie and I worked hard to help him change his thoughts and behaviors. In doing so, he had to finally come to terms with, and work through, the verbal abuse he witnessed his father giving to his mother. Charlie knew he did not want his girlfriend to walk out. Because of his commitment to change, Charlie and his girlfriend eventually walked down the aisle!

Fortunately for Charlie, he learned that it is very hard for your partner to find you attractive when you behave in unattractive ways. How you act usually determines how your partner will react.

Now consider, Chrissy, who was determined to improve her relationship with her husband, which had come under a lot of stress. Here's how she described it:

"Want to talk stress? We have two children and one foster child, a new house, a dog, a sick mother-in-law, and both of us work. Robert and I had really grown apart. We had such little time for each other and there was always something stressful that needed to be dealt with or thought about. So using Jeff's advice, I decided to take one of twelve positive relationship resolutions each week and practice it. What a difference! It made me Mindful of my behavior. I realized that even though we don't have a lot of time together, I can make the time we do have together better by not nagging, listening, and resolving differences quickly. And it's just like Jeff says, 'The more good you do, the more good your partner will do.' This is a great way to stay in tune with your relationship. It worked for us."

Like Chrissy, take one of the following twelve resolutions and put it into practice. When you're comfortable with it and doing it more automatically, add another the next week. Keep adding them until you've incorporated all of them into your relationship. These resolutions are not listed in order of importance; just pick and choose those that apply to you and work on them one at a time. Or think of other resolutions about your relationship. The point is to take positive action to improve your relationship—today.

1. Listen, really listen.
2. Keep a "big picture" mentality.
3. Put your partner's needs above your own.
4. Catch your partner doing things you appreciate.
5. Use "I" statements.
6. Aim to resolve disagreements quickly.
7. Don't bring up the past when dealing with the present.
8. Don't nag.
9. Be spontaneous.
10. Don't trash your partner to others.
11. Don't insult or belittle your partner's work, relatives, or interests.
12. No whining!

Activity #8: Give Yourself Your Own Positive Strokes

When I was twenty-one years old, I was in the first year of my psychology doctoral program. Even though I had all of the outward bravado of a graduate student, I didn't have the discipline and maturity needed for graduate school. I realized this when I received a very disappointing grade on a large research paper. Being a well-adjusted twenty-one-year-old male, I used one of my very prized, highly sophisticated coping strategies—I called my mother to complain and get pity. My mom has always been a huge, supportive fan of mine, with her indefatigable encouragement and endless patience and understanding. I told her how graduate school was really hard and that I was not getting enough positive strokes from my professors. My mother, in her infinite wisdom, said something I did not expect her to say: "Jeff, I suggest you buckle down, try your hardest, and give yourself your own positive strokes."

My mother's words hit me right between the eyes. Yes, I had to be strong for myself and not wait for others to praise me for my efforts. So I share this wisdom with you. Don't get hung up waiting for your partner to give you positive strokes as you go through the effort and exercises I suggest throughout this book. You may get some recognition from your partner up front, and if you do that's great. But also realize that changing thinking patterns takes time. The only person you truly have control over is yourself. Give yourself recognition and your own positive strokes for having the courage to become more mindful, examine your own toxic thinking patterns, and work on your relationship. It's a big deal!

A "PRACTICE IS IMPORTANT" PEP TALK

YOU HAVE A ton of say in the quality of your relationship. I have shared some powerful tools you can use. Trust me, if you work, they work. Years ago I lived with Buddhist monks for a week. It was quite an experience. I was intrigued at how they could, seemingly effortlessly, without any intrusive thoughts or internal distractions, just sit and meditate for hours. It looked so easy! Why was it that when I went to meditate it seemed that within seconds my mind started to wander? I confided in one of the elder monks about my frustrations with meditation. He just smiled and told me how so much of his meditation was about acknowledging outside thoughts and just gently waving them off. He struggled too, yet he accepted that this was part of the process of meditation. He was not perfect, and I did not have to be perfect either. What a relief!

It's common for people to have many unrealistic expectations about relationships. It's common for people to struggle with toxic thoughts about their partners. Don't be like so many people who repeat the mantra "We just drifted apart" while drifting from relationship to relationship. Do the work. Get to know your own mind and stop wishing that your partner could read it for you.

A hopeless romantic believes the fantasy that love is the solution to life's problems. He or she thinks that real love is just there, on autopilot, without needing any active navigating and negotiating. Many people confuse lust with love. There are people who change lovers often. They thrive on the excitement of the initial stages of love. These are just some of the more exaggerated examples that come to mind. Many of us have our own erroneous expectations about love. These expectations set us up for disappointment down the road.

Your thoughts about yourself, your partner, and relationships in general affect your attitudes toward your relationship. If your thoughts are unrealistic, and toxic, you will inevitably be disappointed with your partner. Many people enter into relationships with the expectation that if they find the right person, the relationship will take no effort. This is a totally unrealistic expectation. *Love takes a lot of work.*

In more ways than you may think, we are all the same. We all have deeper layers that hide under our socially acceptable exteriors. If you are unwilling to explore the deeper layers of your thoughts, your relationships will remain superficial and unfulfilling. You will feel that something is missing—that your current relationship, and likely your past ones, were never intimate; that your partners have never understood you; that you cannot understand your partner. You will be wondering why love seems to elude you. Don't make the mistake of thinking that happiness is gained by turning from person to person, looking for the "right" one, because you will never find him or her. You will never create the loving relationship that you desire, unless you are willing to put forth the effort and ongoing practice it takes to discover who you are and who your partner is, and to reveal your true self to your partner.

TO SUM IT ALL UP

REALIZING THE IMPORTANCE of practice will help you maintain the health of your relationship over the long haul. A relationship means togetherness. As a couple, you have chosen to spend your lives united. The two of you travel life's journey together, through its peaks and valleys, so that you can both experience the type of loving, committed relationship we all seek. As individuals, and as part of a couple, we all need to practice the art of loving; in the moment, in the hour, and daily. At all times, the art of loving requires patience, confidence, discipline, concentration, and faith. When you are both practicing the art of loving together, on a daily basis, you will experience a unique, fulfilling relationship that will be strong and resilient enough to endure any problems you may have. Without putting in the work, even the most perfectly matched couple's relationship will eventually fade. Many of us learn this the hard way, regretting that we did not work harder in a previous relationship while we still had the chance.

So my message to you is that practice makes not perfect, but much better. My hope is that you will keep these words in mind as you go forward. Reach down, put in the effort, and keep an open mind. Practice getting to know your own mind. Understanding yourself helps you understand your partner, and this in turn will help your partner to understand you. Nothing feels better than that.

7 Purging Emotional Ghosts: An Advanced Lesson in Beating Toxic Thoughts

I AM A great believer in the power of cognitive therapy. I believe that you can directly change your thinking by becoming mindful of your thoughts and proactive about changing them.

Most cognitive therapists stress focusing on the present—what's going on in the "here and now"—and focus on changing your thoughts from there. This approach works very well with couples. I have found, however, that while rethinking and generating alternative thoughts usually helps couples trying to overcome toxic thinking, it is still important to be on the lookout for those deeply entrenched and hard-to-shake toxic thoughts.

WHEN TOXIC THOUGHTS JUST WON'T QUIT

REMEMBER CLAIRE'S CATASTROPHIC Conclusions about Joel's business venture from Chapter Three? Seeing the evidence that her toxic thoughts were unfounded helped calm Claire's fear of bankruptcy.

However, what if this evidence wasn't enough to calm Claire's fears? Sure, for a few days, even for a week or so, Claire felt lighter without her toxic thoughts, but what if the thought *We're going to go broke* kept haunting her? No matter how much Claire tried to stay mindful of the facts and stick to her alternative thought that she and her husband probably wouldn't go broke, her mental detox through MAP just wouldn't stick.

This happens. For some people, in some situations, it may take additional work to rid themselves of toxic thoughts. The reason is emotional ghosts.

Difficult circumstances and unpleasant things affect all of us. Some of these unfortunate experiences leave a permanent mark on our thoughts and our lives. Parents let us down emotionally and eventually die, peers reject us, lovers leave, and people wrong us. All of these factors can lead to toxic thinking. Out of all of life's uncertainties, one thing is certain: *how you cope with adverse experiences impacts how you think about yourself and the one you love.*

Let me say that you're not about to go on a mission to blame, shame, or devalue your parents, peers, or past relationship partners. You got lots of good things from those who have been in your life. Love, respect, and caring are emotional gifts that you receive from others. In many cases these gifts felt really good and were really good for you. At the same time you received emotional gifts of love from parents, peers, or past intimate partners whose offerings were far short of ideal—yet those people likely did the best that they could.

We commonly hear the word *baggage* attached to difficult circumstances from our pasts. My term for this is *emotional ghosts.* Unresolved problems in your life can haunt you like ghosts. The point is that whether you use the word *baggage* or *ghost*, any one of us can be weighed down by the burdens of unresolved issues.

The good news is that past adversities, and even traumas, do not have to permanently burden your mind. They don't have to lead to uncontrollable toxic thoughts. With self-reflection and a commitment to growth and change, adverse experiences and the consequent feelings can actually be an inspiration to overcome and triumph. It is not your past that determines your future, but how you view your past.

WHERE DO YOUR EMOTIONAL GHOSTS COME FROM?

EMOTIONAL GHOSTS CAN be genetic, for example, a predisposition to anxiety, depression, or an addiction. They can also linger and haunt you as a result of your environment, such as dysfunctional parents, peer problems, or recurrent relationship failures. There may also be a combination of these two types of factors. While the majority of your ghosts come from your past, some can even be created by your present circumstances.

Regardless of the source, dwelling on your past pain and emotional ghosts will hurt your intimate relationship. Here are the three main "closets" where our emotional ghosts hide.

Behind Door Number One: The Ghosts of Family, Past and Present

Imagine being part of a large group of people in a big room. The lights are turned down and everyone—including you—is told just one thing: to listen for a parent's voice from when you were a child. There is no other direction or prompt, just listen for your parent's voice. Whenever I have done this exercise in seminars, I have been amazed at the powerful reactions from the participants both when the lights are off and when they are turned on. Individuals volunteer stories of joy, shame, and pain from their pasts. I often hear stories of triumph, of how people overcame their negative self-images and went on to grow and accomplish things they never had imagined. Whether your emotional ghosts fit on one hanger or are pouring out of your closet, it's never too late (or too early) to examine your ghosts and clean house.

It is well known that the patterns of thinking and behavior by which we express our love toward our intimate partners are largely shaped by our own upbringing. Whatever the circumstances were in which you grew up, you most likely hold strong views on intimate relationship's based on your childhood experiences in your own family.

Once, when I was walking out of a movie theater, I saw a young man in his early twenties walking arm and arm with a young woman of a similar age. The young man suddenly wheeled her and, pointing at her, exclaimed, "How many times do I have to tell you . . . ." I saw his female companion look away sheepishly. I would bet you that this young man was being haunted by the emotional ghost of shame. It seemed very likely that one or both of his parents talked to him in a condescending manner and that he was passing this way of relating to people on to his partner. We are often unaware just how much our childhood experiences affect what we think, say, and do. This is particularly the case in our intimate relationships. How you handle conflicts, your need for personal space, and your willingness to discuss certain topics was likely shaped by your parents or parent figures while you were growing up.

Our emotional ghosts form from the conditional love our parents gave us as children. Maybe you were "valuable" if you made good grades, or you were "irresponsible" because you did not get good grades. Or maybe you were "always thinking of yourself" or were "not athletic like your brother." As adults we tend to seek out what was familiar to us as children. So, despite our proclamations to the contrary, we very often "coincidentally" end up choosing partners who resemble a parent in mannerisms, ways of relating, or even in appearance.

You can't deal with what you can't see. In recent years there has been a marked increase in the percentage of people prescribed antidepressant and antianxiety medications. In many instances these medications are very helpful. At the same time, it is my sense that a considerable number of individuals may rely on such medications to dull the unresolved turmoil of emotional ghosts that continue to haunt them. Don't get me wrong, psychiatric medications can be very beneficial and are also very necessary for some people. My hope, however, is that medications are not used as a way to avoid working through unresolved, difficult issues and feelings from our childhoods.

Many people are not mindful of what occurred in their childhoods and why they still think, feel, and act in less than helpful ways. I think of the breakthrough Ellen had when she finally realized that her resentment toward her husband Isaac for spending time with his son, Ben, from his former marriage, was due to her feeling that she never fit in as the adopted child in her own family. As Ellen and I were able to identify her adoption-related ghosts, she gained new insights into the unfair feelings that she was projecting onto both her husband and stepson. She worked through her own abandonment issues by talking about them and found the evidence she needed to dispute her toxic thought toward Isaac (*He will always pick Ben over me*). Ellen realized that Ben's desire to be close to his father did not have to mean that she was automatically unwanted, unappreciated, or unloved.

Ellen went on to remove her ghosts from her relationship with her husband and was able to accept Ben. Coming to terms with underlying conflicts such as these can take us a long way on the road to true intimacy.

Many people are capable of doing this kind of work on their own, through journalizing, self-reflection, or by confiding in trusted friends. For others, counseling and psychotherapy—especially if you feel you have no one to confide in—can help many work on their childhoods and can be a rich source of insight.

It can be tragic when people are clueless about their family issues, and it is not all that uncommon. I once talked to a psychologist colleague who shared with me that she did not even realize that her father was an alcoholic until she was in her forties—and she even did her doctoral dissertation on alcoholism ten years earlier. Now that's denial!

Behind Door Number Two: The Ghosts from Peers, Past and Present

Carol was an attractive, articulate, and amazingly talented artist and musician, yet she had very little self-confidence. She recounted endless stories to me of being the "ugly duckling" during her growing years. She shared how peers made fun of her for having buck teeth and being overweight and clumsy. These painful experiences persisted well into her middle school years, leaving an indelible mark on her self-esteem. Consequently, she found the need to please virtually everyone in her life. She found that she would try repeatedly to please her parents, her siblings, and her husband, James. But when she would try to please them, she would silently resent it and then undermine the giving, caring things that she had done for others. Carol's peer-related ghosts led her to fall prey to Overactive Imagination, with thoughts like *I'm out of his league, he's going to leave*.

Tired of the turmoil and negativity in her mind, Carol was determined to exorcise her emotional ghosts. She and I examined her painful memories. I helped her to see how she had overcome the negative self-image she had as a child. She was married to a very successful man, was popular in her community, was praised by many as a teacher of both dance and music, and had been asked to audition for a part in a community talent show. Looking at her accomplishments helped her break her toxic thought patterns in her marriage. She no longer looked at James and thought, *He never appreciates me* because she learned how to finally appreciate herself.

As children, our peers play a very important role in helping us to determine how we feel about ourselves. From the time we are young we look to our peers for encouragement and approval. Children have a tendency to be intolerant of differences and peers may mock those who don't neatly fit the mold. Being ostracized by friends or picked on by peers can undermine how you feel about yourself. This, in turn, can lead you to identify these themes of rejection with your intimate partner, even if they are unfounded (as in Carol's case).

I've worked with many individuals who had painful childhood experiences growing up because they were gay. Ryan, age twenty-seven, came to see me because he and his partner Zack were arguing so much that they were thinking about calling it quits. Ryan described his relationship with Zack as the most serious relationship he had ever been in. "Zack is considerate, giving, and understanding," Ryan said, "so why is it I can't stop picking fights with him?"

Ryan told me that in many ways Zack reminded him of a good friend that he had in high school. This person was such a close friend, Ryan felt safe enough to tell him the truth about his sexual orientation. At first his friend was very understanding and supportive, but gradually began to distance himself from Ryan and eventually he just ignored him. This left Ryan feeling very vulnerable, isolated, and abandoned. For the remainder of his high school years, Ryan was depressed.

A few years later, Ryan had sought help for his depression at a college counseling center. It was there that he finally received validation and support as a gay man. Sadly, Ryan's story is a common one. While I have worked with many gay people who have been supported by their heterosexual friends, I have also seen gay clients who have carried the emotional ghosts of feeling betrayed by friends who would not be supportive of their sexual orientation.

Though he no longer experienced depression, Ryan's emotional ghost—his fears of abandonment—kicked in as toxic thoughts when Zack took a new sales job that involved some travel. Flooded with Overactive Imagination thoughts like *Zack is going to leave me; everyone I care about does*, Ryan began to sabotage the relationship by picking fights with Zack. Luckily, Ryan was able to work through his peer-related abandonment ghosts. He and Zack eventually found themselves arguing much less.

Behind Door Number Three:
The Ghosts from Intimate Relationships Past

Intimate relationships bring on the strongest feelings in life—both positive and negative. Romantic love is pretty amazing! It inspires the most powerful, warm feelings (when things are going well) and the most painful, horrible ones you can ever experience (when things aren't going so well). This is because we are so emotionally vulnerable with an intimate partner. We put our hearts and egos on the line. Yet intimate relationships don't always go the way we want, which can leave a whole host of feelings to deal with after they end: sadness, grief, anger, guilt, resentment, and so on. We often find ourselves replaying old conversations and scenes with our ex-lover, wishing we could do them all over again with a new outcome.

Once a relationship has ended, you need time to move through these feelings and reach a resolution. Anger, loss, shame, resentment, and regret, among other negative feelings, need to be expressed in a healthy way. I often advise my clients to write letters to their ex-partners. These letters are not for mailing, but rather for purging the thoughts and feelings that still remain. (One client wrote twenty-six letters before she could let go, but she did let go.)

Anger is usually the most identifiable and pronounced emotion when a relationship ends, but you must keep in mind that underneath the anger are usually feelings of hurt, fear, sadness, and shame. Once the anger has passed, sadness may dominate, and this feeling needs to be adressed as well. Feelings of regret also need to be worked through, so that you don't cling to the hope that your partner will magically return. In most cases, with the passage of time and some emotional work, you are left with the sense that things happened pretty much as they should have, that you learned from those experiences, and that you're ready to move on. You hope that a better relationship will come along, and a new search begins.

Unfortunately, most people skip a great deal of that process. Hurting and wanting to feel better, they rush out and get involved in new relationships too quickly, not realizing that the emotional remains of the past cannot be so easily avoided. One day, the new lover does something remarkably similar to the old lover, and a chain of emotional reactions is set off like firecrackers. Even though this partner is different, the feelings are the same, and it's understandable that your reactions will also be the same. Picture the following scenario:

Elaine's former husband, Kevin, drank heavily and would often arrive home drunk. This led to many upsetting nights, usually ending with an argument of some kind and Kevin passing out. Later, he was defensive, and resentment escalated on both sides until the marriage ended.

Now Elaine is seeing Steve, who rarely drinks. One night, he entertained clients from work at dinner, had a drink with them, and then went to Elaine's. The minute she saw him, Elaine smelled the alcohol on his breath and was immediately flooded with panic, fear, and anger. She fell prey to Catastrophic Conclusions (*He's going to end up like Kevin*) and the *Should* Bomb (*He should know I can't stand him drinking*). Even though she logically knows this is a different relationship, her unconscious mind has already registered the trigger and the feelings from the old relationship come flooding back. If she's not careful, she will find herself picking a fight with Steve, and reacting to him as she was accustomed to reacting to Kevin.

Tim found himself being overly critical of his wife Barbara's weight. He very much respected Barbara but still replayed the memories of his old girlfriend Janet. Janet had told him that he was overweight and not very good in bed. Tim had carried around this ghost of feeling inadequate with women since that time. The ghost would appear in the form of Disillusionment Doom toxic thoughts about the physical attributes of partners, including Barbara. Tim and I took a closer look at the damage he had suffered from Janet's negative comments. He had idealized her as "perfect," which left him perceiving the women in his subsequent relationships as physically inadequate.

WHY REBOUNDING CAN BE BAD FOR YOU

IF AND WHEN a relationship ends, my advice is to allow sufficient time after the breakup of the old relationship to heal and put things back in perspective before starting a new one. This also gives you time to decide what you want in the future. Ideally, people do not move on to new relationships until they have had emotional closure on their former ones. I have to say that in "real life" it does not always work this way. Some people move on to new relationships without much time and effort to grow from the mistakes of the former ones. While this does not necessarily predict the demise of the next relationship, it does provide some serious challenges. Even if you have taken the time to get closure, realize that no matter how much healing time you allow, old feelings and reactions can still intrude on a new relationship. Be prepared for this, and be willing to discuss it with your new partner and ask for his or her support and understanding. Thus, Elaine can tell Steve her feelings about drinking and where they come from, rather than just blindly reacting. And if you feel as though the old feelings are running the show instead of you, seek some therapy to help you complete the old relationship. You'll carry your emotional ghosts from past relationships to the grave unless you confront and resolve them.

THREE STEPS TO EMOTIONAL GHOSTBUSTING

NOW THAT YOU know where emotional ghosts come from, you should have a better handle on the emotional ghosts that haunt you.

Keep in mind that you can be haunted by more than one ghost within the same category, or a number of ghosts across categories. If you tried using alternatives in the way I showed you in Chapter Five and it didn't work, take these steps:

Step One: Meet Your Ghosts

You can't control what you can't see. You need to increase your mindfulness of emotional ghosts that may still haunt you. But should any of the material here stir up emotional unrest of a significant nature and you find yourself depressed, anxious, or unable to sleep or eat for several days, I encourage you to follow up with a qualified mental health professional.

The following exercise can help you become aware of your emotional ghosts, how they still haunt you, and how they turn your thinking toxic. Get a piece of paper and write down unresolved issues that have repeatedly cropped up as obstacles in your family, peer relationships, and past intimate relationships. First, identify the problem in your current relationship so you can look at it clearly and logically. Second, write what really happened in your past. Third, write down why it hurt you. Fourth, ask yourself if this problem occurred in past relationships and how long this problem has been going on.

Here's what two of my clients wrote:

Bart, age 45

Family Ghosts:

Identify the problem in your current relationship:
    I get bored sexually and then I cheat on my partners.

How do you usually (toxically) explain this to yourself?
    She never satisfies my needs. She should know that men need to have multiple partners.
    We have bigger sexual appetites than women.

What really happened in your past?
    My father was unfaithful to my mother.

How did it hurt you?
> It made my mother sad and withdrawn. She used to say men were no good. It made me feel doomed, like I was just like him and I was going to do the same thing.

Has this problem occurred in past relationships and how long has this problem been going on?
> Yes. I have never been faithful to my partners.

Shana, age 34

Peer Ghosts:

Identify the problem in your current relationship:
> I get overly defensive when my husband and I see things differently.

How do you usually (toxically) explain this to yourself?
> He is an egotist who always has to be right.

What really happened in your past?
> I had a group of my peers from cheerleading turn on me when I was in seventh grade. I was asked to leave the squad and since that time I have always been afraid of being exposed for my flaws. The coach sided with the other girls and did not hear my side of the story.

How did it hurt you?
> I felt flawed and defective, like my opinion won't matter and I'll be dismissed unless I get my point in first.

Has this problem occurred in past relationships and how long has this problem been going on?
> Yes. I would label my past partners as defensive because if I gave them that label then it was my way of letting myself off the hook.

Fortunately, both Bart and Shana were able to see how a past hurt was influencing their current thinking. Then they were able to take the next step.

Step Two: Take Your Alternatives to the Next Level

Once you know what your ghosts are and how they contribute to your toxic thinking, you can do something about it.

Arguably, past emotional ghosts impact all of us. But when you have certain experiences from your past that you can't let go, it may be difficult to detoxify your relationship. Consider Claire.

Claire grew up with a father who was anxious about the seasonal ups and downs of his dress shop, which eventually failed when large department store chains became popular. Claire's parents had to sell their home in a comfortable upper middle class neighborhood to pay off the dress shop. They moved in with Claire's grandparents, "who were only too happy to remind my mother that she had married a loser."

While her husband, Joel, had a different "money sense" than her father, Claire had more than her share of Catastrophic Conclusions in response to Joel's plans to start a new business. Claire's fears of being broke and bankrupt were quite reality-based for her. Though that reality no longer existed, her issues of financial security were the "buttons" that got pushed whenever Joel's business venture came to mind. And what appeared when the buttons got pushed? The emotional ghost of her father's business failure reappeared.

Once Claire recognized that "No matter how hard I stay mindful of my better alternatives, I can't stop my toxic thoughts from creeping back in," she was able to see that she was being influenced by something larger than the immediate issue of Joel's business venture. In addition to using evidence to dispute the toxic thoughts, she also needed to gather evidence to dispute her emotional ghost that was feeding her toxic thoughts. After spending some time on her own thinking about it, Claire showed me the following list of evidence:

> Joel is not in the clothing business with its seasonal ups and downs.
> Joel is not like my father was when it comes to finances. Joel is much more conservative about using credit.
> I am not like my mother when it comes to finances. I do not spend money we don't have.

I am no longer a helpless child. I am in a position to contribute to our income once the kids are both in school.

By digging a little deeper into her past, Claire was able to see that her emotional ghost, though painful, was actually rooted by a memory of feeling helpless. She got to the root of the anxiety that was causing her to leap to Catastrophic Conclusions.

Claire was able to review the additional evidence and tell herself, *Joel is a smart guy. If anyone can make it work, he can. And if it doesn't work, we'll bounce back and be okay. Joel is not my father and I'm not my mother. We're different people. This is a different situation.*

Step Three: Be Mindful of Your Ghosts

I'm not saying that you can easily make your ghosts vanish. But once you have identified your ghosts and declared that you will not be ruled by them, it is time to prove to yourself that you can overcome them. Be mindful in this way. Rather than trying to deny you have ghosts, just tell yourself they are only a part of you—they *are not you.* Differentiate yourself from your ghosts by listing how you are different from them. Embrace the qualities that others value in you. Maybe your mother was angry. Take note of how you *are* different from your mother. Remind yourself that she was angry because her father died, the family had little financial resources, and your mother ended up being a mother to her seven siblings. Your life is different— your husband lost his job and you were supportive, not angry. Your daughter spilled soda on the couch and you started to get angry but you caught yourself in a way your mother could not have done.

Once you can maintain this kind of healthy mindful awareness of your emotional ghosts, you can, as Claire did, move on and take your alternatives to the next level—you too can beat toxic thinking.

REFUSE TO BE A VICTIM OF YOUR EMOTIONAL GHOSTS

THERE IS NOTHING wrong with you for wanting to avoid facing the emotional pain of your past or present. Avoidance may *feel* like the right thing to do, but facing your ghosts and dealing with them *is* the right thing to do. Get rid of the idea that you have no control over your emotional baggage—you absolutely do have control over it. The point of exposing your emotional ghosts is not to blame your parents, girlfriend, boyfriend, ex-husband, old friends, or anyone else. And, it is not that these sources necessarily actually abused you, although this may have happened as well. Whatever the extent of the dysfunctional behaviors and patterns you have been exposed, you must remember that you are the one in control, not the ghost. Either you control the emotional ghost or it controls you. There's no one else who can help you out here. If you blame another person, you will feel like a victim. You will learn nothing and be doomed to repeat negative behaviors or perpetuate negative attitudes indefinitely.

Instead, accept responsibility for what happened. Say to yourself (or the other person, if appropriate), "I allowed myself to fall prey to your negative ideas and toxic thoughts about me. But I will not allow you to control me anymore." We all can move on and grow. Just because you rescued your mother does not mean you have to rescue your husband. Just because you were told you were not good enough by your father or brother does not mean that you have to "get back at men" or view them as "impossible" to please. Just because you discovered that you were homosexual and were ostracized by your classmates as a teenager does not mean that you cannot find acceptance as an adult. You *can* overcome your ghosts, no matter why they haunt you.

BUT I'M STILL REALLY OBSESSED WITH TOXIC THOUGHTS

So, what if developing alternatives and working through the hauntings of your emotional ghosts still does not set you free from toxic thoughts?

If this is the case, *do not give up*. Be patient; developing alternatives and working through emotional ghosts may not bring the level of detoxification you are seeking as quickly as you would desire. Some of my clients report same-day results in getting control over their toxic thoughts, while for others it takes months. Typically, the more you practice, the easier and more successful you will be.

In rare cases, I have worked with clients who still cannot seem to break free from toxic thoughts about their partners, even after they develop alternatives and deal with any lingering emotional ghosts. Such individuals may have more serious obsessive thoughts. For these people, searching for the evidence to develop alternatives may actually cause a high degree of agitation, anxiety, and depression.

For a person persistently obsessing with toxic thoughts, it may be helpful to see a qualified mental health professional. In some cases, psychiatric medications can help alleviate obsessive toxic thoughts.

TO SUM IT ALL UP

IN MOST CASES, consistent with the vast success of cognitive therapy for most people, using evidence to develop alternatives to toxic thoughts is very effective. In some cases, looking further back or around you to find lingering emotional ghosts may be necessary to help put your toxic thoughts permanently to rest.

Emotional ghosts do not have to linger and haunt you and your intimate relationships. You can learn from your past pain and move on. Being mindful of these past emotional hurts is the first step to dealing with them. Look for the relationship between your emotional ghosts and your toxic thoughts. Effectively dealing with your emotional ghosts frees you to completely invest yourself in your relationships. Cleaning up, clearing out, and dealing with emotional ghosts is an ongoing process as you continuously embark upon new experiences in your life. What I mean by this is that others may unknowingly (or knowingly) do things that disappoint or even hurt you throughout your life. Becoming "ghost-free" in the face of such disappointments and hurts is not an effortless or automatic process—it requires monitoring and acknowledging your consequent thoughts and feelings. Being open to self-reflection and facing your emotional ghosts, however, will help you to clear them out from behind any closed doors. If you commit to doing this, I am sure that you will become relatively ghost-free.

Dealing with the negative stuff in your life is crucial for effectively moving on and being able to form healthy intimate relationships.

Some people seek out chaos and find ways to be busy all the time, but this is no way to successfully deal with your feelings. Avoidance of this kind will set you up to keep repeating the same destructive patterns. Your childhood may not have been perfect, your past relationships may have disappointed you, but you don't have to suffer for the rest of your life. The good news is that you *can* get some degree of closure and acceptance and move on. But, ultimately, no one can give you closure and acceptance but you. No one can free you of your toxic thoughts but you. Though the work may be difficult at times, the payoff is huge!

8

The Nontoxic Glue That Holds Your Relationship Together

RELATIONSHIPS HAVE A glue that holds them together. It may surprise you that this glue is not love. It's empathy. Empathy is the power to understand and imagine another person's feelings.

I have never had someone come into my office and say, "My problem is that my partner understands me too much." Developing empathy for your partner means really understanding what life has been and is like for him or her. Empathy is not some mystical power. It is not magic, intuition, or the "warm fuzzies." And make no mistake; empathy is not mind reading. But, as you will soon see, it may just be the next best thing to mind reading in relationships.

Hold on a minute. Let me clear up a point of common confusion—empathy is not the same thing as sympathy. Sympathy is when you feel badly for your partner or you're sad for your partner if something bad happened to him or her. Empathy, on the other hand, is being able to actually understand your partner's perspective or situation to the degree that you can identify with what they are feeling and why. If you sympathize, you feel for someone because of his or her pain. If you empathize, you feel his or her pain with them. For example, Kate doesn't just sympathize with Brian because he had a difficult childhood. She is able to imagine what it must have been like to have had a chronically ill mother and a depressed and withdrawn father. She understands that Brian, given his family problems, lived with considerable uncertainty. Brian's way of coping was to become extremely self-reliant—to the point where it was, and is, difficult for him to ask for help from others, including Kate. Kate's empathy for Brian and his childhood problems empowers her to look beyond her own needs and to avoid overly personalizing Brian's need to work out problems for himself. Empathy is the cushion of understanding that helps to absorb any bumps in the road for Kate as she relates to Brian.

Empathy is not something that drains or depletes partners. Sympathy can be draining, but empathy cannot. Sympathy leads us to feel that we *have* to do something. Empathy empowers us by providing a special sense of togetherness and connection that is formed by powerful, mutual identification for the one you love.

So loving someone automatically means being empathetic with them, right?

Not necessarily. According to *Webster's New World Dictionary and Thesaurus* (2nd ed.), the term *love* can mean: 1) strong affection or liking for someone or something, 2) a passionate affection of one person for another, 3) the object of such affection, a sweetheart or lover, and, last but not least, 4) tennis, a score of zero.

Based on these definitions and my own experience working with couples, love does not necessarily include empathy. When it comes to intimate relationships, no matter how much love there is between you and your partner, there's no guarantee that you both will be able to automatically empathize with each other—even if you think you're "soul mates."

ANOTHER GOOD REASON TO DETOXIFY YOUR RELATIONSHIP

ONE OF THE worst things toxic thinking does is that it paralyzes your ability to empathize with your partner. If you're busy thinking things like *He should know how important this is*, and *She's going to wreck the car like she does everything else*, it's hard to understand and accept your partner in an empathetic, supportive manner.

Toxic thoughts put a tremendous drain on empathy. The Three-D Effect—Distraction, Distance, and Disconnection—makes empathy difficult. It's hard to imagine how someone feels if you're emotionally distant. Toxic thoughts by nature are "me-focused," as in how your partner is failing you in some way, *He's overreacting again just like he always does!*. Toxic thoughts that remain unchallenged lead you to erroneously assume you know your partner's point of view. When you think toxically, you assume negative things about your partner's intentions and even his or her value as a person. Toxic thoughts are explosives that blow apart bridges to understanding.

Tony and Anne are a prime example of how toxic thoughts can create dangerous, empathy-busting assumptions. Tony had a mistress. Not in the classic sense but, for all in intents and purposes, just as damaging as "another woman." Tony's mistress was his career. He was "married" to his law firm. Anne had successfully developed many outside interests over the course of their twenty-five-year marriage. With the book club, tennis lessons, and horseback riding, along with every school committee under the sun, Anne found herself in a very paradoxical position: She had a "full plate" of activities, yet she was starving for a nourishing, satisfying emotional connection with Tony. Tony, unbeknownst to Anne, who was trapped in her toxic thoughts, *He never wants me, he is workaholic who will never change*, was hurting as well. He dreamed of love and closeness with Anne, but he was clueless about how to get it. Lost in his own toxicity, Tony thought, *All she cares about is the kids and her activities. I've never really mattered to her.*

I helped Tony and Anne overcome their toxic thoughts. I coached them to challenge these thoughts and truly listen to one another—empathetically. It took a lot of work. I helped them see a reason for staying together other than pursuing their separate passions and sharing children. This couple did get closer. Not light-years closer, but enough to make a positive difference.

Toxic thoughts are exaggerated and inaccurate distortions that get in the way of you seeing things from your partner's perspective. By learning to identify and counter your toxic thoughts with more reasonable alternatives, you have already overcome the first roadblock to empathy. Couples whom I help to overcome toxic thoughts almost immediately report a growing appreciation for the issues and concerns of their partner. This is such a common phenomena that I've now coined a term for it—The Law of Reverse Momentum. Think of toxic thoughts as a "not-so-merry-go-round." Left unchallenged, toxic thoughts will continue to spin through your mind with ever increasing momentum. It is exciting for me to see couples who can reverse the spinning craziness of toxic thoughts. They find that they literally start to turn in the opposite direction, toward empathy, compassion, and support—hence the name The Law of Reverse Momentum—once they rid themselves of toxic thinking and open themselves to walking in the other partner's shoes. With The Law of Reverse Momentum, you will discover how much you begin to see the world through your partner's eyes. You see more and more of your partner's challenges and concerns and you appreciate them in a way that makes you feel closer, more appreciative, and more supportive.

For George, The Law of Reverse Momentum kicked in as he detoxified his thoughts about his fiancé, Elizabeth. George lived on his own and felt that Elizabeth *Never wants to spend time with me like she should want to. After all, I am going to marry her.* As George weighed the evidence, however, he realized that Elizabeth had made a lot of emotional and physical space for him in her world. He became more and more cognizant of the time constraints Elizabeth faced in shouldering the demands of her children from her first marriage. He realized that his needs, and at times demands, for her time were unrealistic and that she was actually quite accommodating to him. This was just another example of how getting rid of those toxic thoughts paves the way for the road to empathy.

SEVEN MORE ROADBLOCKS TO RELATIONSHIP EMPATHY

TOXIC THINKING IS not the only roadblock to empathy in your relationship. Once you're free of toxic thinking, make sure you are also free of these seven other behaviors taken straight from my work with couples who have had trouble empathizing with one another:

1. Talking too much

I'm amazed at how many people just don't get this: *It is hard to open your ears and your heart if your mouth is wide open and flapping away.* Here's an important piece of advice for you: If you talk less, and listen more, you will be more empathetic. Your partner will respond very positively to your increased listening and empathy. Aside from literally biting your tongue, one way to help you talk less is to first ask yourself what your statement is constructively going to accomplish. Being mindful of the true value of what you're going to say will help you be more judicious in choosing how to relate to your partner. In many cases with couples, I have seen that less truly is more. (See page 141 for listening-enhancing activities.)

2. "I'm right, you're wrong"

You can't be supportive of your partner's case if you can't see past your own viewpoint. The "I'm right, you're wrong" mentality robs you of being able to truly connect with your partner. Life has a way of humbling all of us. I remember Rob, who entered into therapy with his second wife years ago. Angry and defiant, he was frantically gesticulating to his wife about why she was "always wrong" and how he was "always right." My best supportive, yet firm efforts to help Rob see that it takes two to make a relationship work or fail were met with his frustration, and he quit therapy. Rob bumped into me three years later at a grocery store. He looked sheepishly at me, took me aside and informed me that he was now on his third divorce. Rob asked me if I would help him with his "personality hang-ups." Rob learned a hard lesson about "I'm right, you're wrong."

People who have a strong need to be right or always to win find their capacity to be empathetic very limited. Empathy means looking beyond your own sense of self and being able to experience the emotional world of your partner. The "I'm right, you're wrong" mindset shuts down the partner on the receiving end—his or her viewpoint is dismissed. He or she is not correct and that's all there is to it.

As I've gotten older, I've realized that despite all I know and have experienced, there is much more to learn and experience than I could have ever imagined. I try to keep this in mind in my relationships. Every once in a while I'm tempted to think or say, "But I'm right," or "I know this." Yet when I step back from things, empathize and reflect, I often realize that the issue is not about right or wrong and what I do or don't know. It is about realizing that there are different ways of looking at issues and new experiences. Being empathetic, therefore, helps us work out misunderstandings with our partners with openness, compassion, and flexibility.

3. Fixing it can break it

The third barrier to empathy is feeling you have to "fix" or solve your partner's problems. Men are typically more guilty of this than women. Resist the urge to solve the problem and just truly try to understand it. I saw this conflict come to life with Shelli and Francis. Shelli simply wanted her husband of twenty-two years to hear how she felt now that their oldest daughter Samantha was leaving for college. Francis, who was proud of his ability to solve problems (he was a highly successful president of a large company), kept offering ideas on local schools Samantha could attend instead or what Shelli could do to visit more or keep herself busy. On and on he went, plowing right over her feelings of loss.

People who feel they have to "fix it" often mean well. But the reality is that people who are "fixers" are usually trying to avoid their own sorrow and pain and prevent these feelings in their partners as well. Some partners who want to fix things don't like to acknowledge pain because it makes them feel helpless. I have seen big "aha!s" from "fixers in recovery" who now understand about how just listening and empathizing can be very empowering for their partners.

4. Going through the motions

Just going through the motions and not being sincere is also a serious obstacle to empathy. Hollowly reassuring your partner is not empathy. When Stewart told Sheila, "Honey, you're not fat," he believed he was being empathetic. However, Sheila was fifty pounds overweight and really needed Stuart to empathize with her frustration about not losing weight, and not simply try to smooth over this reality. Though Stuart loved his wife and wasn't as bothered by her weight gain as she feared he was, he was not providing Sheila with the kind of support she really needed. When Stuart was finally able to empathize with his wife's issue, he was able to be supportive in a way that truly mattered and was helpful to Sheila.

5. "We're just too different"

The whole principle of empathy is seeing from your partner's point of view. But if you have certain ideas or values that are very different from your partner's, you may think, *We're just too different.* This kind of attitude really can get in the way of empathy. For example, you may have different ideas about privacy. For Fred, privacy meant sharing his marital conflicts with his friend Steve. For Louise, Fred's wife, privacy meant that all their personal challenges were not to be shared with any outsiders, even family members. By helping both partners learn to accept their unique upbringings and personality styles, both Fred and Louise were able to become more empathetic, and far less threatened, by their different takes on privacy. As Louise became more empathetic toward Fred, she was able to see that his need for outside support from others helped him to shed the negative messages he heard from his mother growing up—(that he was "fat and lazy and would amount to nothing"). As Louise shared with Fred how she now could really understand his needs for outside validation, an interesting shift occurred—Fred no longer had such a burning urge to run and discuss with outsiders how he felt when Louise disappointed him. This was because Louise's newfound empathy left her (and Fred) feeling less threatened and more able to open up to one another.

We've all been on the receiving end of empathy. It feels really good, doesn't it? Think of the teachers and bosses for whom you worked the hardest for. Chances are, you felt they connected with you and powerfully understood you. We feel motivated when we feel understood. Our intimate partners, just like you, feel motivated when they perceive that they are understood. The ability to understand another person is invaluable in every human relationship. I have seen incredible positive changes occur between fathers and sons, mothers and daughters, siblings, and intimate partners who learn and apply this critical skill.

6. Denial of our own pain and suffering

When I see clients who are in denial of their own pain, it often propels them into denial of their partner's pain. To develop real empathy for your partner, you must at one time or another permit yourself to feel frightened, overwhelmed, or helpless. Your own sense of strength comes from embracing your own sense of vulnerability. Similarly, being empathetically strong for your partner and being able to identify with his or her sense of vulnerability is rooted in accepting, and not denying, your own pain and vulnerability.

Unfortunately, many people think that because they are afraid or have pain and anguish, it makes them less attractive to their partner. If you buy into this mindset, you will be reluctant to share what is bothering or upsetting you with your partner. Remember, however, what I said back in Chapter One: "what you resist will persist." Your pain won't go away and your partner is likely to feel that something is wrong.

Tasha's "never let them see you sweat" mentality is a good example of how an unwillingness to embrace your own pain can block empathy. Tasha lost her job and tried to deny to her husband, Manuel, how much it really upset her. Tasha told herself that she needed to be strong and not share how she felt betrayed and hurt by her job loss. Tasha actually was afraid to show Manuel how upset she was because she felt she would really "lose it." Besides, she felt that Manuel would be disappointed in her if he discovered that she was weak and felt like a loser. "He always said he loved how strong and resilient I am."

Manuel, a sensitive, open man, felt Tasha growing increasingly distant toward him. As many people do, he personalized her withdrawal, jumping to the Catastrophic Conclusion that she was not happy with him. Finally, when Tasha reached out to Manuel, they both felt a tremendous sense of relief. Manuel discovered the real reason for her emotional distance. She discovered that Manuel, who had lost a job before they met, was a tremendous support for her. "He really understood my pain and my feelings," Tasha said. "I don't know how I would have gotten through [this] without him."

Your partner cannot empathize with your pain if you're not willing to recognize it yourself.

7. Too much empathy is dangerous

Overempathizing can be dangerous. It can lead to burnout or to Emotional Short-Circuit. If you ever had the misfortune of having a dead car battery, you may have had someone "jump" it. This involves running a cable from the car with the dead battery to one with a live battery that has "juice" to spare. Once the dead battery is charged and revived, the cables must be removed or the electrical system on the second car can short out. Following this analogy, the concept of codependency occurs when one partner loses him- or herself to the desires of the other partner. There is only so much energy to go around. If you are overly emotionally invested (enmeshed) in your partner, you leave little energy and resources for yourself. A classic example of this dynamic is when one partner who has an active addiction and the other partner is so supportive and understanding that she neglects her own needs and then burns out.

HOW TO BE MORE EMPATHETIC TO YOUR PARTNER

SO ARE YOU born with the ability to empathize or do you acquire it? The answer is most likely both. Within the field of counseling and psychotherapy, empathy is thought of as both a skill and a trait—if you're not currently empathetic, you can learn this skill.

Therapists typically are trained through rigorous empathy-enhancing activities, with stress role-playing and other perspective-taking exercises. Empathy is also taught among many prejudice-prevention and tolerance-enhancement programs. And we train children with empathy-loaded statements, such as "How would you feel if someone walked up to you and took your favorite toy?"

The following four activities can help you develop empathy and understanding for your partner and vice versa. Remember, empathy begets empathy. The more you put out the more you will get back. When we feel uniquely and accurately understood, it puts our emotional ghosts back in the closet where they belong. This leaves us less defensive, less toxic in our thinking, and more emotionally available to be empathetic with our intimate partner.

Activity #1: Where You're Coming From

We can know so much about our partners and yet not know just as much at the same time. Even though you may have known your partner for several years, don't assume you know everything about him or her, especially about his or her emotional ghosts (he or she may just become aware of them). Many of us, especially men, are taught at an early age to deny or hide our pain.

The prompts below are designed to help you become more empathetic toward your partner by putting yourself in his or her "place." The goal is simply to shift your viewpoint temporarily to your partner. Ask yourself the following four questions. (Write down your answers):

1. My partner's challenges in growing up were _____.
2. My partner's biggest fears are _____.
3. What my partner needs most from me is _____
   _____.
4. My biggest obstacles for my partner are _____
   _____.

Now, share your answers with your partner, who has asked him- or herself the same questions. Ask your partner to let you know how you did in assessing his or her challenges or her obstacles. If you find a discrepancy, use this as a chance to learn about your partner. You can't be empathetic until you really know what's going on in his or her head.

Activity #2: Swap Your Shoes

That's right! This activity helps you both learn what you each sound like—from the person with the other point of view. So, take off your shoes and have your partner take off his or hers. Now put on each other's shoes. This may look and feel weird, but I'd like you to sit directly across from each other and do a reverse role-play of who you each are and what you each are usually concerned about.

Go ahead and get really into it. Assume your partner's voice and mannerisms. It's okay to laugh. Chances are that it will be funny. But *don't* make fun of your partner. (Some couples even tape-record it and play it back when they're through.)

Now ask yourselves the following questions and share your answers:

* What did you each learn about one another?
* What were you most surprised to hear?
* What would you like to hear instead of what you heard?

When couples do this exercise in my office, it can be very eye-opening. Cindy and Dan discovered some very important things they had not previously known.

Cindy: "It was not until I listened to Dan pretend that he was me that I realized that at times I do talk to him like he is one of my employees. It's funny, our decision for me to be the bread-winner was a mutual one, yet I was not aware that Dan still has some awkward feelings about staying home with the kids."

Dan: "This exercise was helpful because it gave me a structure to really express to Cindy what it feels like for me when she gets into corporate mode around the house. I know she does not mean it, but sometimes I feel like she talks down to me. Just putting that out to her and her really hearing me helped me get past some of my toxic thoughts like, *Here she is, Miss Corporate Hot Shot, always thinking it has to be her way.*"

James and Keri found this shoe-swap exercise to be very enlightening as well. Both were feeling very frustrated after four years of infertility workups and procedures, without any positive results, when James asked Keri to swap shoes with him.

James: "Doing this exercise helped me appreciate how often I had been nagging Keri about following all of the fertility clinic specialists' suggestions and whether or not she got her period each month. Hearing Keri's frustration as she played out the way I keep checking in with her gave me a newfound appreciation for how I come off very demanding in my need to know."

Keri: "This exercise also helped me appreciate how it must be hard for James when I shut down and just don't want to talk about our fertility situation. I really got to see how helpless and stumped he feels."

Activity #3: Read Your Partner's Feelings

Okay, you know by now that you can't read your partner's mind and that he or she can't read yours. But you *can* sometimes gain a better understanding of how your partner is feeling by tuning into his or her body language. Couples who are good at reading each other's body language and gauging each other's feelings can be empathetic with one another more easily.

But the tricky thing about viewing body language as a window to your partner's emotions is that people will often say one thing but really think and feel something else, and usually this difference is communicated in their body language. We are all guilty of doing this, at least once in a while. For example, you may say, "Sure, honey. I don't mind if your mother comes on vacation with us," but your crossed arms and sarcastic tone are saying, "No way is she coming with us."

Now that's an obvious example. Many times, couples are not as good at reading the more subtle emotional cues given off by their partner's body language. You may be aware that what your partner is saying is not really what she means, but are you so sure you do know what she means?

Debbie and Tim met with me ostensibly to discuss issues with Tim's daughter Kim from a previous marriage. Kim was caught in the middle of a vicious custody battle between Tim and his ex-wife. Tim described his current marriage to Debbie as "really good" and "very strong" though strained because of the custody battle. Yet, Tim seemed oblivious to how Debbie leaned away from him as they sat next to one another on the couch. He was also oblivious to the pained expression in her eyes. When I gently probed Debbie about what she was thinking and feeling she shared her pent-up disappointments and frustrations about her relationship with Tim. She felt like the custody battle was hiding their marital shortcomings.

Debbie was doing what many people do in relationships; she was expressing her feelings nonverbally and expecting her partner to automatically understand the meaning. (Again, a wish for mind reading.)

Tim was doing what a lot of other people do—missing the cues. Helping Tim read body language and helping Debbie understand that this may not be an easy task for Tim has greatly helped their relationship. One of the ways I was able to help both Debbie and Tim was by having them do the following activity together. Even if you think you're good at reading your partner's feelings, you may be surprised.

Directions: Look at the list of feelings below. Pick one and write it on a 3" x 5" index card. Take turns with your partner and try to express that feeling without words. One partner observes and the other one is the actor. Use any expressions, body positioning, or gestures. The observer tries to guess the feeling the actor is attempting to express. When the observer has guessed the feeling correctly, switch roles and start over. If the observer has not guessed the feeling correctly within two to three minutes, the actor finally tells the partner what the feeling was, and then the actor and observer switch roles. Repeat the exercise with three to five different feelings.

List of Feelings

- sadness
- jealousy
- anxiety
- shock
- joy
- distress
- pity
- fear
- disappointment
- happiness
- frustration
- affection
- hysteria

- delight
- grief
- love
- pain
- panic
- anger
- surprise
- compassion
- guilt
- impatience
- exhilaration
- boredom
- loneliness

Now, answer these two questions:

1. What did you learn about how your partner reveals his or her feelings?
2. What did you learn about yourself?

Many couples, like Debbie and Tim are surprised to discover how inaccurate they could be in reading each other's nonverbal cues. Debbie felt deeply offended with Tim for sitting with his arms crossed when they were talking about her mother's recently diagnosed Alzheimer's disease. She held in her negative feelings driven by the toxic thought, *He is just a closed-minded person. He doesn't care what I'm going through with my mom; even his body language demonstrates that!* It was not until Debbie expressed her concerns with Tim that he told her that he did not know he was acting closed off and that this was not his intention. In fact, much to Debbie's surprise, Tim was able to empathetically reflect back to Debbie, with accurate understanding, her concerns and feelings about her mother. Tim then shared that he remembered having chills at the time and was sitting with his arms crossed to keep himself warm.

Activity #4: Practice Truly Listening to Each Other

People in relationships often complain (toxically) that their partners *never* listen to what they say. Lorraine and Charles had this problem when she came home and announced that she'd made a decision to see a friend's allergist to deal with her nagging sinus problems. Her husband Charles was blown away and almost jumped through the roof. "I've been telling you to see an allergist to help you with your constant sniffling for years. Now all of a sudden your important friend Lorraine tells you and you finally listen. Why is it that you never want to listen to me?"

Clearly, Charles was riddled by All or Nothing toxic thoughts. When I worked with this couple, I was able to help him detoxify. He challenged his All or Nothing assumptions and realized they were just not true. Lorraine often did listen to him.

As Charles stepped back and looked at Lorraine without his toxic thoughts, he also came to a startling realization. Yes, he had repeatedly told Lorraine to see an allergist, but his advice was unsolicited, and he'd been giving this "suggestion" to Lorraine in an intense, pressuring way. Lorraine had wanted understanding and empathy, not advice. *He can* never *listen to me. Why does he always have to tell me what to do*, she had stewed to herself.

Charles's advice was helpful, but his method of delivering it was not. The couple learned a powerful lesson about empathy and how to support one another by accurately listening and understanding the other's true needs. Active listening is essential to promoting empathy. Charles had been good at giving advice, but not at active listening. An active listener does a lot more than just wait patiently until it is his turn to speak. An active listener:

- hears his or her partner's words.
- notes the emotional tone of the words spoken.
- observes the body language and gestures that go along with the words.
- is mindful of the signals he or she is giving with their own body language and gestures.

- reflects back to his partner what he or she said.
- expresses appreciation for what is shared with him or her.

AN EXERCISE IN EMPATHETIC LISTENING

DO YOU WANT to give this empathy stuff a shot? Below is a simple yet powerful three-step exercise for couples wanting to develop greater closeness through empathetic listening. Again, the purpose is not for me to train you to be a mind reader, but rather to increase your capacity for empathy as a couple. All you and your partner need is to have a sincere desire to become more understanding of one another.

The object is for each partner to describe a concern from his or her point of view hoping that the other partner will understand it better. There will be a talker and a listener. Once the exercise is completed, switch roles so each of you has a turn to be both the talker and the listener.

Step One: Be a Mirror

The talker expresses a concern and the listener demonstrates an understanding of that concern. To do this, the listener acts as a "mirror" by repeating each word of the concern. Keep in mind that by repeating the concern, the listener is not necessarily agreeing. The listener may have a different view on what is being said, and yet still mirror effectively. The talker should limit statements to a length that the listener can remember and repeat. Once the talker has fully expressed the concern, the listener summarizes it and the talker acknowledges the summary's accuracy. If the listener's summary is not accurate, the discussion continues in the same expressing/listening format until the talker acknowledges the accuracy of the summary. Again, the concern of the talker can make sense to the listener even if the listener does not agree with it.

A Note of Caution: Listeners, keep your guns in your holsters. It is natural for the listener to want to respond right away to the talker's concern. Don't let any toxic thoughts grab you and derail you from this process. As a listener you must quiet any urge to react, knowing that the roles will soon be reversed. Repeating may seem artificial, however, it is of great value for the talker to know that he or she is being heard. Again, the listener must resist reacting to the concerns of the talker and instead genuinely ask, "Is there anything else?" This provides an opportunity for the talker to share more deeply.

Step Two: Actively Empathize

To empathize means to have some understanding and to identify with your partner at an emotional level. The listener tries to understand what the talker is feeling. The listener must use a "feeling" word, like *angry*, *hurt*, *satisfied*, or *happy* (remember, you can share positive experiences and feelings, too). For some partners it is easier to use a metaphor that expresses a feeling; this is also okay. You could say, for example, "I felt like I had a ton of bricks on my chest" or "I felt like a mirror that had been smashed to bits." Don't react defensively in either role. Emotions can be difficult to grasp. Couples should take enough time to find emotional agreement.

Step Three: Express Appreciation for Being Understood

Don't go rolling your eyes at this suggestion. By doing this exercise you see firsthand how challenging it can be to truly listen and understand where you are each coming from. So honor your willingness and your partner's willingness to do this exercise. Understanding one another—deeply and accurately—takes time to master and is an ongoing process. By completing this exercise you have taken a huge leap forward. Reinforcing these positive steps is a very important habit to cultivate. Too many times, partners get in a rut, telling one another what they do "wrong" instead of what they do "right." I don't like the words *right* and *wrong* when it comes to relationships because they reflect All or Nothing toxic thinking. But I do like the idea of reinforcing appropriate and positive behaviors. So for Step Three I'm asking you to say two words to your partner: "Thank you."

EMPATHY TAKES TIME

DON'T EXPECT THAT just because you want to be empathetic toward your partner, it will happen overnight. But if you remain mindful that empathy is the glue of successful relationships, it eventually will happen.

I often think of Gus and Belle as a good example of how empathy can bring back a couple from the brink of separation and give the partners a renewed sense of commitment and determination.

Gus grew up poor in rural Texas with nine siblings. As a child he was determined "to make something" of himself. Belle met Gus in college and was immediately attracted to his "go-getter" style and determination. They married, and for the first five years, life was good and their relationship was solid. After their first child, David, was born, however, things seemed to take a turn for the worse. David was colicky and Belle and Gus were exhausted by his inconsolable screams and their constant lack of sleep. Their fantasies of smooth sailing with David did not turn out to be the reality. Two years later came their next child, Daniel, later to be diagnosed with learning problems. During this stressful time, Gus "lost" himself in his career and eventually founded his own large corporation. Belle had all the material possessions she could ever want but felt alone, isolated, and overwhelmed meeting the children's needs. Gus would leave the house each day at 6:00 A.M. and come home at 7:30 P.M. Aware of Belle's discontent but unsure of what to do about it, Gus would check his e-mail and voice mail immediately upon arriving home, and then plop down in front of the television. Belle felt Gus did not want to be with her. Gus resented Belle because their sex life was not what it had been during the first five years of their marriage. Gus saw sex as a way to reconnect. Belle felt sex treated her like an object for Gus to use as a physical release.

In their first session, they explained their problems as *We just drifted apart*. I told them my theory about how pieces of wood drift apart but couples do not. There is always much more to it, often involving toxic thoughts. Belle had toxic thoughts about Gus, such as *It is all about him, I can't depend on him at all to be there for me*. Gus thought, *She has no interest whatsoever in sex and she never will.* Empathy between this couple was lost.

I worked with them individually for a while. It was not easy. In fact, during one session I shared my thoughts with Gus on the value of acceptance and forgiveness, he stormed out stating he could never forgive Belle for withholding sex. Gus came back, however, and really began to work on appreciating Belle's perspective and how she felt emotionally abandoned by him. He also looked at how he saw sex in a conditional way, *If she gives me sex then I'll do things for her.* Belle worked on seeing things from Gus's perspective. She realized that his angry style blocked him from expressing how he really felt: scared and vulnerable.

After three months of counseling, this couple experienced a huge shift. They both came in smiling one day. Both stated they were doing much better and feeling more optimistic than ever. I asked what had happened to allow them to make such a positive turn. They initially smiled and stated that they weren't sure. I couldn't let them off that easily, and I explained the importance of really understanding what occurred to make things better.

Belle said, "Gus really gets it. He understands me in a way he never did before. It's not that I have no sex drive, but that I craved to feel connected to him emotionally."

Gus said, "Well, she really gets it now, too. Belle sees that my angry barking was really about my fears that she did not find me appealing or attractive. She sees how much I love her, but how clueless I was about how to connect with her. I thought being the breadwinner was what I was supposed to do, but there is much more to it than that."

Gus and Belle were finally able to become empathetic. In addition to sorting out and challenging their underlying toxic thoughts, they also realized that their differing conversational styles made for some challenges when they were listening to one another. Boisterous, overlapping talk equaled rudeness for Gus, which led him to emotionally short-circuit. In contrast, loud talk meant enthusiasm and passion to Belle. Belle wanted details, but Gus felt interrogated when Belle would seek more information. Belle wanted to talk things over at length, and Gus just wanted to get to the point.

Being sensitive to each other's different communication styles will not be a quick fix. Both partners need to be attentive and tolerant of each other.

Because Gus and Belle worked to understand each other, they were able to finally have their breakthrough. To help nurture this breakthrough, I coached them on performing random acts of kindness for each other (see page 173) and really listening to each other (see page 188). They lost their agree/disagree mentality and shifted to a mindset of mutual understanding and acknowledgment.

Yes, it took a few months, but considering Belle's and Gus's fifteen years of disconnection, they were able to rediscover each other in a way they never had before. It was very gratifying for me to see the incredible power of empathy at work for this couple.

ONE FINAL THOUGHT ABOUT THE POWER OF EMPATHY

A LOCAL HUMAN services director asked me to do a series of workshops on the topic of emotional safety. Since I liked the agency and the director, I agreed before I had a chance to research the subject. Of course, I found little in professional literature that specifically addressed emotional safety.

Immersing myself in the subject, I quickly began to appreciate how safety is a fundamental human need as described by the work of Abraham Maslow, a highly accomplished psychologist and personality theorist. For Maslow, *safety* meant security: protection from physical and emotional harm. Examining the emotional aspect of safety for this training, I realized that empathy is at the heart of emotional safety. Empathy helps create emotional safety by affirming that our struggles are okay—not necessarily right or wrong, but okay. This helps us to let down our own negative judgments and barriers. When you felt "safe" as a child, you explored your surroundings. When you felt "safe" in the classroom, you raised your hand without fear. When you feel safe in your relationship, you can express your emotional needs and be true to them—that's emotional safety. And it's a beautiful thing!

TO SUM IT ALL UP

All too often, couples therapists can become referees for their patients. In these situations the focus is on which partner is going to change what behavior. This focus, based on toxic thoughts, can quickly backfire.

Time and time again, I have found that helping partners to understand and accept each other is much more helpful than one party trying to convince the other who is "right." Understanding and acceptance leads to empathy. There's no denying it—detoxifying your thinking is greatly enhanced by learning how to be empathetic. I have found that when partners stop making demands like *You need to stop patronizing me* or *You never clean up after yourself*, and instead truly learn how to acknowledge each other, positive change is more likely to occur.

Remember, empathizing with how another person feels does not have to mean you agree with him or her. You are simply acknowledging the other person's feelings and giving him or her the validity he or she deserves. You can say, "You know, I don't agree, but I can totally see where you're coming from." Think about how good it feels when you feel understood without judgment. Your empathy is one of the greatest gifts you can give to your partner.

I often describe empathy as "emotional glue" for couples. I also think of empathy as a bridge that connects one partner to the other. Each of you grew up with your own unique experiences and expectations. Being empathetic is the best way to bridge your differences. This bridge, when strong, can withstand the inevitable stresses on the relationship, including the demands of children, time, work, and finances. In a truly mutual intimate relationship, a partnership of shared understanding, partners are stimulated and energized by genuinely empathizing with one another.

The Eight Rules
for Fighting Fairly

IF YOUR RELATIONSHIP suffers from toxic thinking, I can practically guarantee you that you and your partner have not been fighting fair. Toxic thinking promotes toxic fighting styles (*He should know how I feel about this by now. I'm so mad I'm going to leave and not tell him where I'm going!*), and toxic fighting styles promote toxic thoughts (*Here she goes again with the door slamming. She's totally out of control!*).

As you can see, unfair fighting is a vicious circle, one in which many couples are caught. A vehicle that should promote understanding between couples instead becomes a disaster area!

Does any of the following sound familiar? Be honest! Have you or your partner ever:

• • •

- wanted to (and sometimes did) go ballistic (yelled, threw things, slammed doors) just to make your point or get your partner to pay attention to what you were saying?
- given the other partner the silent treatment or walked out on him or her?
- hurt your partner (with sarcasm, name-calling, label slinging, or button pushing) just so you can have the last word?
- held grudges and later used them against your partner (revenge)?
- had the attitude, *If I don't get what I want, I will quit cooperating?*
- expected the other to do things your way or "take the highway"?
- pretended there's no problem at all because it's easier that way?

If you answered yes to any of the above, you're not alone. Most people never learn conflict resolution skills and most people get emotional when fighting with their intimate partners. That's a bad combination.

However, by reading this book, increasing your awareness about toxic thinking, and giving MAP a try, you've already taken important steps to start fighting more fairly. That's because as you work through the three steps of MAP, you can't help but fight better with your partner.

And the rewards keep pouring in. As you continue to detoxify your thinking, you will discover a dramatic and even immediate improvement in the way you handle yourself during conflicts with your partner. First of all, you won't have as many conflicts. As you dispute your toxic thoughts and replace them with more reasonable ones, you won't be as likely to jump to conclusions, have unrealistic expectations, or lose your temper if you do have a conflict.

Secondly, you'll be able to stop yourself before things get out of hand. So if you do slip up (we all make mistakes now and then) and let fly a toxic label, like "You're such a loser," or an All or Nothing toxic statement, like "You can't ever do it my way," you'll be able to do damage control, like Sue did.

Sue: "I was doing great and being mindful of my toxic thoughts until Max and I got into a big fight. Up until then, I had been able to catch myself before it was too late. But this time, I lost myself in anger and I did an Emotional Short-Circuit by yelling: 'There's something wrong with you. Normal men don't act like this.' The second it came out of my mouth I regretted it. I held up my hand and I said, 'Wait a second. I'm very sorry I just said that. I know that what I said was mean and untrue. That was an old habit talking. Will you give me another chance?'

"Thankfully, Max was willing to drop it and give me another chance. We went on to resolve our issue much more peacefully than we had started out. My stopping and apologizing was the right thing to do."

Like Sue, you need to remember that as you recover from toxic thinking you're still vulnerable to relapsing during the heat of an argument. It is when you are faced with conflict that you need your mindfulness skills the most. Your emotions are high and your logic is absent. When you are sad, angry, confused, or disappointed, it's easy to *Should* Bomb (*He should know me by now!*), Emotionally Short-Circuit (*I'm done with you; you're a nut case!*), leap to Catastrophic Conclusions (*Our credit is now down the drain!*), or play the Blame Game (*If it weren't for you, my dreams would have come true.*). Such toxic behavior does not allow you and your partner to fight fairly because you see each other as adversaries—the one who is at fault, the one who should change, the one who should know better, etc. When this happens, you become stuck at the same frustrating point in every effort to make decisions and solve problems.

HOW MINDFULNESS CAN HELP

REMEMBER THAT HAVING toxic thoughts and engaging in negative behaviors like slamming doors or yelling does not mean that you are a bad person or that your relationship is doomed. It simply means that you are not a perfect human being and that sometimes you act in self-defeating ways. By admitting this, you can target and then work to control toxic thoughts and try to eliminate specific self- and partner-defeating actions. By improving yourself in this way, you will increase your chances of solving problems with your partner. Again, mindfulness goes a long way in helping you keep your cool.

Here are several guidelines for maintaining mindfulness during an argument with your partner:

- Monitor yourself to avoid using toxic language that may be perceived as provocative or insulting to your partner. Stick to those "I" statements rather than "You" statements. For example, instead of "We would not have been late had you not taken so long to get back here," say, "I'm really upset by how late we are." Be on the lookout for All or Nothing language ("always," "never," "just once") or Label Slinging ("couch potato," "money drain," "shopaholic," "workaholic").
- Before you say anything, repeat what the other person said as a way of clarifying potential areas of misunderstanding. You may be ready to "hit the ceiling" over nothing.
- Keep focused on the here and now. Slipping into conflict over past issues can derail even the most caring of couples. Sometimes we do not recall the details of past conflicts, nor do we have any control over the past. Stay in the present; otherwise, you'll only get sidetracked.
- Never try to resolve conflicts in front of others. You might not mind, but often third parties are uncomfortable witnessing the private issues of another couple.
- Stay mindful that only one problem at a time can be solved. Avoid shotgunning, or the practice of unloading several problems at once ("And while we're at it, how about when you told my mother to mind her own business"). This only serves to confuse the issue and often results in limited closure on the central concerns.

If you haven't been fighting fairly, you're going to love the results when you start to fight in a more positive way. But it will take some adjustment for both partners. Most of us are not prepared for a calm, timed, rational approach to problem-solving. But conflicts are a part of daily life, and you can learn excercises like the ones above to resolve them.

EIGHT RULES FOR BREAKING THE VICIOUS CYCLE OF UNFAIR FIGHTING

ONCE YOUR TOXIC thinking is under control, you will be in a much better position to follow and stick to what I call The Eight Rules to Fighting Fair. When you follow these rules, you will be empowered to resolve your conflicts and keep your fights fair and productive.

Rule #1: Think Rationally Before You Speak

Gloria is a petite woman in her fifties, with a gentle, self-effacing manner—unless she is angry with you. She told me, "Bernie says he's going to leave me if I can't get my temper under control. But I can't. I don't know what happens to me when we argue. I know I should think before I speak, but I can't. I just lose it and say all sorts of mean things."

When we become angry or fearful, we don't actually "lose it." We get a surge of adrenaline; we feel "pumped up," and our bodies react accordingly. As you now know, your toxic thoughts can cause strong physical reactions. In the face of conflict we may feel some strong, unusual, and discomforting feelings. Just feeling your chest pound or hearing your voice quaver can be alarming. And, not surprisingly, the more the issue seems important, the more intense our physical reactions will be. The body's way of managing this stress is to initiate a fight-or-flight response. While this can be beneficial in dangerous situations, these automatic reactions may not lead to effective and thoughtful decision-making. We may feel ourselves become anxious in various ways (increase in heart and breathing rate, queasiness, dryness of the mouth, muscle tension, or tightness in the stomach). If voices are raised, some people feel sadness or fear, while others experience rising anger. These are normal responses to what our bodies think is a threat. Here's what you can do to control yourself so you don't go ballistic or say things that you will later regret:

- Take at least three or four slow breaths, breathing in through the nose and out slowly through the mouth. Don't underestimate the power of breath to quickly calm you down.
- Say to yourself, _____ is someone who cares about me and I care about him(her). I'm not going to demean him (her) by behaving badly.
- If you're still not calm, count to ten. This actually works by removing your instant response to blurt out something toxic.
- Remind yourself that feeling "pumped up" is normal. You're experiencing the body's normal way of dealing with what is initially perceived as threatening and stressful.
- Consciously stand or sit in a relaxed posture.
- If you feel you are becoming very sad or angry, tell your partner.
- Excuse yourself from the room to collect yourself.
- Respect each other by keeping a reasonable distance and avoiding physical touch that may be interpreted as condescending or prematurely intimate.

Rule #2: Commit to No Toxic Behaviors (Yelling, Slamming Door, Etc.)

I told Gloria, "If you want to maintain your relationship with Bernie, no more raising your voice or slamming doors."

"But . . . ," Gloria tried to interrupt.

"No 'buts,'" I told her. "You must not consider these negative behaviors as options."

"But," Gloria protested. "I just can't."

When my clients claim they can't help it, I tell them, "I don't buy it." Then I use my "presidential" argument. I ask them how they would behave if the President of the United States were nearby when they were upset. Or, if that visualization is not working for you, ask yourself how you would act if you were cornered by an assailant brandishing a loaded gun. Would you be rude to some crazy person threatening to shoot you? My guess is that you would probably not. The bottom line is that if you can pull it together for those people and special circumstances, you can do it at other times for other people—especially for your intimate partner.

Getting control of negative behaviors is also important because they may be interpreted as intimidating or elicit defensive behavior from your partner. Gloria saw me for an individual session after she had just returned from visiting her elderly parents in New Jersey.

She said, "Jeff, I have to tell you something. I went to see my parents this weekend because my father is having one of his depression episodes where he is just full of gloom and doom. My mother started to scream at him and act hysterical. I never realized it before but that's what I grew up seeing. I guess I thought that was the way I *should* treat Bernie. Then it finally hit me; what you were saying never sunk in until this last visit when I saw my parents in action. My theatrical flair when I go crazy on Bernie makes me just like my mother with my dad. I decided you were right and I simply must learn to control my temper. So I have counted to ten and lowered my voice with Bernie, and he is actually listening more to me. Your suggestions really work."

I just smiled at Gloria and said, "Go figure." We both laughed. Two years later I received a call from Gloria telling me that things were better than ever between her and Bernie.

Rule #3: Argue for Resolution, Not to Win

This one is important: Don't try to be the winner of an argument. In relationships, it really isn't whether you win or lose that's important. It's whether or not you treat each other fairly and with respect. Being right is about perceiving yourself as more powerful than your partner. Don't become a four-year-old child. Think about how partners regress when they think about winning and nothing else. Mindfulness of the partnership is the all-important key to remembering that, when it comes to relationships, trying to win means trying to fail.

Couples who are involved in a struggle over the balance of power between them usually are trying to prove "I'm right and you're not." A couple locked in a powerful struggle can disagree over anything and everything—even a game of backgammon can become a major skirmish.

The key to avoiding a destructive conflict is to keep in mind that the goal is to defeat the problem rather than your partner. Discussions that involve personal attacks have little chance of producing positive results. One or both partners may try to win using personal attacks such as bullying, verbally abusive comments, or even whining. I think of Alex and Rita as an example. This young couple was divided and embroiled in conflict over the rights of Alex's dog. Rita was not a dog person and Alex very much loved his dog. For Alex, allowing the dog in all areas of the house, on the bed, and in the car felt natural. Rita found the dog's free reign to be entirely unacceptable. Rita felt that she did not matter and that Alex "values the dog more than me." Both partners were shaming and attacking one another in attempts to "win" the disagreement.

Happily, Alex and Rita were able to reach some compromises after both partners reframed the situation in terms of how to compromise and best meet everyone's needs, including the dog's. Once the emphasis on winning was past them, the couple came up with an innovative solution: The dog was able to sleep at the foot of the bed, not on the bed. Alex could have the dog in his car but not in Rita's. And the dog could not go in the living room, which they agreed to section off with a gate.

Rule #4: Learn to Give Helpful Criticism

When couples argue, criticisms often fly. When you were still a toxic thinker, constructively giving and receiving criticism in your relationship was probably difficult. If you think about it, toxic thinking is really toxic criticism about what your partner is doing to fail, disappoint, or hurt you. Toxic thoughts, therefore, stack the deck against constructive criticism. Toxic thoughts are destructive in nature.

But here's another piece of good news. Criticism does not have to mean automatic friction, hurt feelings, or the start of a major war. When handled well, criticism can become a way for both partners to get their needs met. When you are mindful of doing all you can to respect your relationship, and when you make a commitment to keep your toxic thoughts in check, you may actually find that criticism is a helpful tool for meeting the valid needs of your partner. When the criticism is delivered in a supportive, respectful way (such as "I have a hard time talking about how I feel when you cry" instead of "You're such a crybaby"), and in an atmosphere of love and security, it can actually increase intimacy. On the other hand, destructive criticism which is delivered in an accusatory manner erodes emotional safety —this can eat away at intimacy.

Criticism is tough for many couples to take because of a physiological phenomenon called *flooding*. Flooding is a term used by John Gottman, a leading couples researcher, in his book *Why Marriages Succeed or Fail*. According to Gottman, flooding is the tendency to feel overwhelmed in response to negative actions or behaviors—both your own and your partner's. You experience a "system overload" and are suddenly swamped by distress and upset. I believe that toxic thoughts are the major cause of flooding. And, as stated by Gottman, when you are flooded and feeling out of control, constructive discussion is impossible. This is similar to what Daniel Goleman, a leading researcher on emotional intelligence, meant when he described the term *emotional hijacking*. Like flooding, an emotional hijacking is an intense bout of emotion that derails your ability to think logically and problem-solve successfully. Emotional Short-Circuiters in particular have a low threshold for flooding because of their limited capacity to "sit with strong emotions," likely stemming from a combination of their own individual temperament and the enviironment in which they grew up.

Listed below are some important guidelines for giving and receiving constructive criticism. Follow these strategies and you will keep the emotional floodwater at bay.

WHEN GIVING FEEDBACK OR CONSTRUCTIVE CRITICISM

Do:

- Approach the subject at a good time. The second your partner comes home is not a good time to criticize.
- Question your motives for criticizing your partner. In the big picture, does the fact that she leaves the kitchen cabinets open really bother you enough that you want to make an issue out of it?
- Focus on your partner's specific behaviors, not his or her

whole personality. For example, you don't want to say, "You're just no fun." Instead, get specific by saying, "I've noticed that you don't seem to enjoy parties. I do, so can we talk about how to handle this difference?"

- Mention positives. This is a huge omission most couples make. Try framing the above issue positively by saying, "I've noticed that you don't seem to enjoy parties, yet you're such a friendly and outgoing person."
- Give your partner a chance to explain or offer feedback. This is a two-way process.

Don't:
- Offer any ominous preambles, "Okay, we really need to talk. There's a huge problem we need to resolve."
- Act and then think. This will provide short-term release, but can cause deep regret later on.
- Play amateur psychologist. Giving your partner your unsolicited analysis of his or her underlying motives can really shut down communication, even if your interpretation is accurate. No one wants their own emotional ghosts turned against them. For example, Denise told her husband Craig, "I think you're insecure because my promotion makes you feel like you don't deserve me anymore, which is just like your father always felt with your mother." Denise later acknowledged she said this when she felt angry and that she knew it was not accurate and was damaging to Craig.
- Make comparisons: "You are just like your father (or brother or sister)." This can influence your partner to feel unfairly labelled with the negative qualities of another party. You can also bring up more emotional ghosts by doing this.
- Make "you" statements. If you say, "You are impossible to talk to and you just don't listen," your partner will feel defensive and justifiably so. "I sometimes find it difficult to be honest with you" is a much more positive way to broach the subject.
- Be sarcastic or unkind with your criticism. You will cause your partner to shut down instead of opening him or her up to your suggestions.

Do:

- Listen with an open mind. One of the biggest qualities that hold us back from personal growth is an unwillingness to see our faults. Your entire personality is not on trial.
- Go with "Ready, Aim, Fire" instead of "Ready, Fire, Aim." Too often we react instantly instead of reflecting on what we hear.
- Ask for specifics so you know which of your behaviors upsets your partner.
- Ask for clarification if needed. Partners on the receiving end of criticism often avoid such probing. What you may not realize, however, is that getting to the deeper issues will more likely diffuse rather than intensify the negative feelings, because your partner will feel understood.
- Understand the issue(s) in the context of the other person—be empathetic.
- Offer solutions. Set up specific easily monitored ways to track progress. Show your partner that you are willing to follow through.
- Thank your partner for being open and taking the risk to give you feedback.

Don't:

- Interrupt. You can't listen if you're talking. Hear your partner out.
- Yell or otherwise act out in response.
- Make excuses or get defensive.
- Deny the feedback. Think about how frustrating it is when someone negates what you have to say.
- Try to match your partner blow for blow. I have seen couples trade volleys of spoken toxic thoughts, particularly All or Nothing thoughts. Avoid these criticism wars—nobody wins.
- Address more than one concern at a time.
- Shut down. Instead, be a grown-up. Don't withdraw and pout, it is very unattractive.

- Get passive-aggressive. Clanging plates loudly after you hear the feedback is not going to help things.

Rule #5: Respect Each Other's Styles and Personalities

Some people get frustrated if they don't get a speedy resolution to an argument. Other people need time to digest and then reapproach the issue. He likes time to calm down before trying to resolve matters, she needs a resolution right now. She likes to make jokes when confronted with problems; he gets deadly serious. He likes to get input from friends; she is very private. What do you do if your personalities are different and these differences are getting in the way of resolving your problems?

We've all heard that differences make the world go round. Yet why is that when it comes to intimate relationships, if our partner does not see things our way or respond in the way that we may think he or she *should*, it's the end of the world? I mentioned earlier how some highly distressed couples, clueless about their underlying toxic thoughts, often say, "we just drifted apart" when they are facing the possible or actual end of an intimate relationship. It is equally disheartening to hear, "We're just different people." When I hear this I usually respond, "Good, I'm glad you're different; can you imagine how confusing and frustrating things would be if you were the same person?"

You need to remember that when you got together you likely had some of the same differences you have today. Why do different styles and personalities have to be a "do or die" obstacle? They don't. Yet, Disillusionment Doomers tend to focus on expectations that are not met and on the differences between themselves and their partner. Label Slingers also get tunnel vision when they don't get their way: "He's so anal." The good news for Disillusionment Doomers, Label Slingers, and anyone else who gets concerned about differences between themselves and their partner is that differences don't mean that you can't fight fairly or resolve your issues. You simply need to respect and work with your partner's style. Take Tom and Jane, partners with very different outlooks. Tom's Mr. Spock-like analysis as he listened to Jane's impassioned, powerfully delivered commentary was not necessarily a bad thing. By not thinking toxically, Jane got herself to a place where she could see some value in Tom's approach. She reframed Tom's "steady at the helm" style as "solid and reliable" rather than "emotionally unavailable."

Instead of trying to change your partner, accept that he or she is likely trying his or her best and wants to be better just like you do—even if he or she has a different way of going about it.

You have to meet each other half way sometimes. Katherine and Ray have learned to do this. Though she likes immediate resolution and he needs time, they've learned to adjust.

> Katherine: "As long as Ray doesn't make me wait for a whole day before talking about what's going on, I can deal with it. He understands that this is hard for me, but that I'm trying. We now have an agreement that we won't go to bed mad at each other, but that doesn't mean we're going to go to bed with a solution either."

Rule #6: Identify Your Own Contributions to the Problem

In addressing a conflict, you are saying to your partner "*we* have a problem." When you accept some responsibility for the problem, your partner perceives a willingness to cooperate and probably will be much more open to the discussion. You may think a set of circumstances or a problem really *is not your fault*. You may feel that your partner is the source of a problem and not you. My response to this is that you *do* have a role in every problem. Take an honest look at yourself and you will find that you play a role—wittingly or unwittingly—in supporting your partner's actions, whatever they are. Remember, relationships have well patterned "dances" that occur between partners. Any problems between you and your partner are a result of your combined dynamic.

As you consider how you are going to discuss the problem together, here are some practical steps to follow:

▸ Take responsibility for the problem; remember, both people are always responsible. When bringing the matter up for discussion, be sure to approach it in a positive ("we have a problem") way and not an accusatory way ("you have a problem we need to fix.") Here is an example: "I have a problem. I have something that is a little difficult for me to talk about, but our relationship is very important to me, and by talking about this problem I feel that we will have a better relationship. I feel that _____ is the problem, and this is what I am contributing to it. I would like to hear what you think and how you feel about it."

- Restate the problem to make sure you have correctly understood your partner. You can't own up to the fact that you're not helping around the house if you don't understand how your actions affect your partner. Ask for specifics.
- Ask for time to think about it. Many times couples leave my office hurt and angry. Yet, most of them return with new insights or a new willingness to own up to their part of their problem. Integrating a different perspective in your mind can often be difficult. We tend to get comfortable with our ways of thinking and to shut out other perspectives that don't immediately fit into our perspective. Consequently, your mind creates a sense of dissonance (psychological tension) as it attempts to make room for new or different information. You have likely been surprised at yourself in the past for coming around to new or different points of view than you previously ever held. Bearing this in mind, be patient with yourself as you work through issues and experience tension or even emotional pain; you will eventually arrive at new levels of understanding.

Rule #7: Be Willing to Make Concessions

"But we can't get to a solution."

You can—even if it's an eventual compromise on both sides. It's important for you to realize that some problems are not easily resolved. It could be that the timing, setting, or other circumstances make it difficult to concentrate or negotiate. Sometimes partners may just feel worn down and not have the energy and focus necessary to reconcile their differences. Once toxic thinking is removed from the relationship, it's often much easier for couples to reach a resolution, even in the most challenging situations.

An example of a challenging conflict is the one between Chhaya (Hindu) and Danny (Catholic). Married for three years, they had described their relationship as "Just the usual kind of conflicts about division of household labor and how to spend money." Now that their first child was on the way, however, conflicts arose about their different cultures and how the child would be raised. Each of them had toxic thoughts about the other:

Danny: She always has to win.
Chhaya: He's out of control about this.

Like Chhaya and Danny, once you are able to overcome your toxic thoughts, there are four positive steps you can take:

Step One: Brainstorm. Try to think of as many solutions to the problem as possible. These should be behavioral changes both for yourself and for your partner. It is important to propose more than one alternative. The greater the number of possible solutions, the more likely you will find one that both of you will accept. Writing down your ideas can help you keep track of them. Chhaya and Danny came up with the following ideas:

- Raise our child as both Hindu and Catholic.
- Raise our child as Hindu since Chhaya is more involved in her religion than Danny.
- Raise our child as Catholic if Danny makes a commitment to attend church and participate.
- Raise our child as Hindu and the next child as Catholic.
- Raise our child as neither religion—let him/her decide upon coming of age.

Step Two: Evaluate the Alternatives. After identifying all of the possible alternatives, evaluate them and make a choice. Your evaluation of each alternative should include: (1) how you would actually implement it, and (2) the possible outcomes. What will be required for each person to implement a given alternative? How will the change affect the behavior of both individuals and their relationship? Again, writing down your ideas can help you keep track of them.

For Chhaya and Danny, the only solution that withstood the evaluation process for them was to raise the child as Hindu.

Step Three: Come to a Mutual Understanding. If one partner likes a certain solution but the other finds it unacceptable, discuss the reasons. Mutual sharing can promote growth and prevent feelings of rejection on the part of the partner who suggested the alternative. Continue discussing each solution until you agree to try one to see if it works. Try to understand your partner's point of view.

Though Anthony and Wendy had at first agreed that remaining in their current neighborhood made sense, Anthony felt a growing sense that moving to a new neighborhood would be best after all. This prompted him to ask Wendy to hear his new perspective on their residential situation.

Anthony: "I wanted us to make decisions as partners. Wendy and I really have been blessed with lots of good things that occurred while we lived here. At the same time, I've been thinking more and more that with favorable interest rates and the better educational opportunities for the kids at this new school district, I became open to moving. In fact, I really now wanted to move, even though this is a new position for me. I'd certainly wanted to have Wendy feel supportive of this. I made an effort to contain my new excitement about moving, because I know I can be intense and come off demanding when I get new ideas into my head. I knew that laying out the reasons to Wendy and giving her time to hear me out and digest things was important to the whole process of discussing it."

Wendy: "Anthony understood that I had to go though a process of seeing the new development a few times and that I needed to visit the new school. In the past he'd knock me over with his enthusiasm, but he did not do it that way this time. He was patient and this empowered me to embrace his excitement rather than shutting down and feeling threatened by it."

Step Four: Give It a Try. In other, more immediate situations, such as one partner's promise to help out more around the house and the other's promise to be on time more often, concentrate on your own behavior changes and allow your partner to do the same. After you have made your behavior changes, evaluate their effect on your relationship. Sometimes conflicts also reflect more serious differences in core values or growth of the people involved. When a solution that contributes to the well-being of the relationship cannot be acheived, it is wise to seek consultation with a counselor or trusted, objective third party. A third party that is objective and caring can often help clarify underlying concerns or assist in identifying an issue that may be causing a blockage. To seek help is a compliment to the value of the relationship.

And don't worry; most problems can and do eventually reach a resolution.

But what if we follow the rules and still find it difficult and frustrating? Remember, I told you this relationship stuff is not always easy. Sometimes you can follow all seven of the rules and your problems still aren't resolved on the first attempt. Perhaps emotions are too intense or the circumstances appear too complex for an easy resolution. It is important to remember that it may take time to think through the issues.

Danny: "One of the things I always looked forward to as a dad was that I would get to make Christmas special for my boy or girl. I wanted to buy lots of presents and go to Midnight Mass together. Christmas was not a happy time in my family because my parents were poor. I wanted the chance to make it different for my kids."

Chhaya: "I don't want Danny to have to give up his dream. We never celebrated Christmas together, but that doesn't mean we can't start now. I'm willing to get a tree and gifts and to participate in the nonreligious aspects if it makes him happy. I also want our child to understand both of our cultures. That's important to me, too."

Try out your compromise or solution. You've got to see if what you've decided upon works. Obviously, this will be a long process for Chhaya and Danny. They may not know if this is a solution that works until their child is of sufficient age to participate in his or her religion. The point is to be open and flexible. Be willing to implement new solutions if the first solution you try isn't working.

Make sure you both feel empathy. When at an impasse, it's important to consider your degree of empathy toward each other. It's no accident that the chapter on empathy precedes this one. Without the ability to understand your partner's viewpoint, it is hard to get through conflicts. Remember, empathy is the glue that holds your relationship together. Empathy helps you to experience one another as a couple instead of two different people. Empathy keeps the sense of "we" alive. This common purpose and sense of "we" helps you to overcome conflicts that cause friction. I often suggest that couples experiment with some empathy-promoting exercises to gain insight into their partners' perspective, like the excercises I describe in Chapter Eight. You can also try the following ideas when you feel stuck:

- Shift gears and call for a "time-out." This is a rest period that allows for each person to have some physical and emotional space. It's important to establish a time to come back together. Failure to schedule this rejoining time may otherwise appear to be a slight or disrespect to your partner. Remember, it only takes one person to call a time-out.
- Be aware of your surroundings. Take into consideration the time and place of the conflict. Perhaps a change in time and location is merited before the discussion continues. It is also okay to contract for time limits on the discussion for any given session. When May and Steve were having an argument about money while staying with May's parents, they realized that they felt too constricted to really get into a discussion. They agreed not to bring up the subject until they got home and had privacy.

- Make sure you have all the facts. Try to be informative but not judgmental with your findings. Lance and Helena disagreed over what materials could go into their new compost pile in the backyard. Helena asked Lance how he would feel if she went on the Internet to get further information. Lance said that would be okay and told Helena that informing him about her efforts to get more information helped him be less defensive and more open to what she had to share.

- Examine your own motives for the conflict. Are there attitudes or beliefs that you can temporarily suspend to better understand your partner's perspective? Austin realized that his negative views about owning rental properties needed to be put on the back burner so he could listen to his second wife Greta's reasons for wanting to keep her townhouse and rent it after they planned to buy a house together. Putting his initial objections aside, Austin realized that this would significantly add to their monthly income and also provide them with a growing asset.

- Consider using an objective third party. If you become stuck and find it difficult to reconciliate, a consultant can provide a helpful perspective.

Rule #8: Forgive

We often are encouraged to forgive, but aren't really told how. As long as you're bogged down with toxic thoughts, it is hard to forgive. A valuable benefit of being mindful and challenging toxic thoughts is that this promotes forgiveness. Forgiving your partner does not mean forgetting; it means that you are accepting your partner in spite of past hurts and disappointments. I'm not saying you should take forgiveness to an extreme and condone repeated abusive or unacceptable behaviors. What I am saying is that forgiveness is necessary in any successful intimate relationship. Forgiveness will give you a sense of inner peace that will create more peace and serenity in your relationship as well.

"HEALTHY BATTLEFIELD" RULES

WHAT'S THE DIFFERENCE between a discussion and an argument? In a close relationship, you will have disagreements. Here is a summary of the differences between fighting fair and fighting unfair.

Fighting Fairly	Not Fighting Fairly
Each person is allowed to make his or her points and then will try to understand the other person's points.	Each person ignores the other person's points.
Each person listens to the other's point of view.	There is no listening. Each person is talking or yelling, often at the same time.
Each person respects the other's styles.	The issue is derailed by stylistic differences.
Focus is on the current problem.	One or both partners brings up past issues and hurts.
Both people speak calmly.	Loud voices, yelling, and other toxic behaviors are used.
Both partners use "I" statements.	"You" statements are used to accuse and blame.
It's not about winning.	Each person wants to win at any cost.
Both partners' feelings are considered.	One or both partners' feelings are put down or ridiculed. There's no empathy.
Brainstorming leads to possible solutions.	There is no brainstorming. Each person insists that there is only one possible solution.
Each person wants to reach a solution that satisfies both people.	Each person insists that his or her solution is the only answer.
A mutual decision is usually reached.	No decision can be reached.
Both partners take action to implement the solution.	One person may take action, but the other won't. Or, both people fail to follow through.
There is forgiveness.	One or both partners holds a grudge and/or engages in the Blame Game.

The Eight Rules for Fighting Fairly   167

Here is a quote by the famous Dutch theologian Henri Nouwen about forgiveness. I want you to hang on your wall or tape to your refrigerator so you can read it every day:

"Forgiveness is the name of love practiced among people who love poorly. The hard truth is that all of us love poorly. We need to forgive and be forgiven every day, every hour—unceasingly. That is the great work of love among the fellowship of the weak that is the human family."

IT TAKES TWO TO FIGHT FAIRLY

Be patient; fighting fairly is easier said than done. At the same time, the more you are mindful of fighting fairly, and the more you practice the strategies I have shared, the easier it is to make it happen. If your partner is dragging his or her heels and just not cooperating, be sure to:

- Admit when you are wrong or have made a mistake. You should certainly do this when you clearly dropped the ball (forgot to pay a bill, left dishes in the sink, etc.). Don't make excuses. Fessing up will diffuse any anger from your partner.
- Be generous in acknowledging "your piece," even if you don't think you should. This suggestion follows an assertiveness technique called *fogging*, where you look for some aspect of truth in what the other party is saying. Admitting your faults influences your partner to lower his or her defenses and often to "own" his or her faults, too. Jody found this helpful with her husband, Mario: "He was all revved up for an argument, but I told him that he was right about me being responsible for forgetting to renew the car registration. My jaw dropped when he said, 'It's okay, honey. Actually, this one is on me because the more I think about it, I now remember saying I would do it.'"
- Agree to disagree. Sometimes couples just reach an impasse where they are deadlocked in intractable, opposing

views. In many cases, both partners may have reasonable support for their differing points of view, and neither one wants to compromise. The best solution here is to agree to disagree. Often what happens is that over time, as emotions settle down, one or both parties will reevaluate their position. Chhaya and Danny were able to work out which religion to raise their child. Yet, they respectfully agreed to disagree on whether to turn an extra bedroom into a playroom or an office. They agreed to put this decision off for six months and then reevaluate.

- Use the "Look what we are doing" tension-breaker. If things really heat up and your partner is locked into unfair fighting mode, firmly but calmly call attention to what is really going on in the moment. When Roberto kept going on and on about whether he should or shouldn't go to Cindy's class reunion, she said, "Roberto, we're just getting very angry at each other and not getting anywhere right now." This broke the tension and allowed the couple to realize that a "time out" was the best strategy for the time being.

- Refuse to engage in toxic thinking or toxic behavior. Even if your partner is stuck in a toxic place, that doesn't mean you have to go there. The only person you can change is yourself. Hopefully, your new and improved fighting style will inspire your partner to change for the better, too.

- Consider professional help. If, after several attempts of trying to "fight fairly" and following the rules and guidelines presented here, you still find yourselves "stuck" at an impasse, or if one of you will not attempt to resolve your differences in respectful ways and slips into "I win, you lose" behavior, you should consider entering couples counseling. No, I'm not just suggesting this because I do this for a living. I suggest it because it can help you work together as partners instead of adversaries. One couple who came to see me admitted that they were worried that I was going to make them sign up for a year of therapy. It doesn't work like that. Some couples can get a lot of good work done in a short amount of time, even a few weeks or months.

Others need more help. Seeing a couples counselor also doesn't mean you're on the brink of something bad, like divorce. Far from it. The couples who get help when they need it are the ones who stay together. Yes, in many cases, couples counseling can be expensive. Yet, the emotional and financial expenses of unnecessary breakups and divorces can far outweigh any costs of counseling. And there are some therapists and counselors who will work on a sliding scale based on your income, if that's a worry. Churches and synagogues often provide free counseling to members. There are options no matter what your situation.

TO SUM IT ALL UP

REMEMBER THAT EVEN the healthiest relationships experience conflict at times. Even if you never have a toxic thought and you are completely mindful of the value of your partner and your relationship, you will still have conflicts with your partner. In every relationship there are stylistic differences between partners and decisions to be made. One partner may be more financially conservative and one may be less so. One may be more lenient as a parent and one may be more strict. The list can go on and on. Couples usually find that differences in perspective and opinion do exist.

What relationship conflict comes down to is that partners do not always think or behave alike. But this does not have to spell disaster. Most of us are raised to think that conflicts are a bad thing, but they don't have to be. Actually, well-handled conflicts can lead to constructive decision-making and increased intimacy.

Maintain your mindfulness of your toxic thinking and follow the rules for fair fighting and, I promise you, you will soon reap the benefits—you will have fewer disagreements, speedier resolutions, and no bad behavior to regret later. Now you can't argue with that!

10

Eleven Ways to Stay Back in Love

THESE COUPLES ACTIVITIES come straight out of my office for you to apply. Once you become familiar with them, you can adapt them to best fit your particular situation. Be open. Try out these activities; some of them really are fun. Some are very simple and require very little effort. As you're completing them, tune in to both yourself and your partner.

You might be thinking, *No way! My partner will never try these things with me.* But you may be pleasantly surprised if you make the offer. If you have a reluctant partner, my advice is to avoid making these activities into a chore. Don't turn them into a huge commitment issue, like "If you really cared about me, you would do this." Instead, say, "I think it will be fun. Let's give it a shot and if we don't like it, we can stop."

One caution I have for you and your partner is that any of these exercises can be either used constructively or as a "set up" for a conflict.

Obviously, my hope is that you and your partner will try these exercises in earnest and with a spirit of patience, mutual support, and respect. Have flexible, realistic expectations and go for it!

Activity #1: Imagine You're the Stars of a New Reality Show

Following through on your new nontoxic behaviors is critical to your commitment to practice your new relationship skills. Here's an exercise that should get your attention. Imagine that you and your partner have been selected (along with two other couples) to star in a new reality show about the ordinary lives and interactions of couples. This means that all of your interactions with your partner are being filmed by hidden cameras all over your house, in your car, and wherever the two of you go.

Whenever you interact with your partner ask yourself, *Would I want other people seeing this?* How would you feel if the entire country observed you yelling, being passive-aggressive or manipulative, or giving the silent treatment? Would you be the couple that others admired or would you be the one whose bad behavior everyone talked about?

I have found this technique really helps me stay honest in my interactions. It works for many of my clients. Here's how it worked for Courtney:

"When Jeff first mentioned this little exercise to us, I thought, *That's for other people.* But I said I would try it. That night I lay in bed and thought about how many of my interactions with Donald [Courtney's husband] I would want to see on TV. I had to admit that I wouldn't want most of them to be seen by others. The next day, I made a point to be aware of how I was acting with Donald and to ask myself, *Would I want other people to see me right now?*

"Wow! This simple little exercise made me aware that I don't always speak to him nicely and that sometimes I get impatient. It really helped me get the point Jeff made about being mindful of what occurs in the relationship. Since doing this exercise forced me to be more mindful, it really helped me change the way I interact with my husband. It makes me really tune in and pay attention to how I act and react. I use it less now, but from time to time I check in with myself to make sure I would want to be on the reality TV show for all the country to see."

Activity #2: Practice Random Acts of Relationship Kindness

All too often, couples simply forget to be nice to each other. I would bet that many people are nicer to total strangers than they are to their partners. In fact, I've worked with couples who have practically kept a log of "I did this for you, so now you have to do that for me." This is very negative relationship behavior. Scorekeeping inevitably leads to resentments. Why keep score if you don't feel somehow cheated?

There is a lot to be said for doing "little things" for each other. Little random acts of relationship kindness can foster intimacy and show empathy. You certainly can do these if your partner is feeling down or is having a bad day. But remember, just being kind for no reason can work wonders in bringing you closer.

Here is how a random act of kindness brought Dana and Sean closer:

> Dana: "I hate to go grocery shopping. It's just one of those chores I would rather not have to do. But because I'm the one staying at home, I accept that every week it needs to be done. One day, when Sean had come early from a meeting, he saw my list on the refrigerator. For some reason, he grabbed my list and said, 'Let me go and do this. I don't mind.'
>
> "I was really taken aback. Here he had just finished up a big two-day meeting at work and I knew he had to be tired. But he offered anyway, just to be nice. Maybe someone who isn't married with kids wouldn't understand this, but that kind offer, out of the blue, meant the world to me. It made me feel appreciated and taken care of. In turn, it made me want to do something nice for him. It touched off this flurry of niceness between us. I would get up and get him a bowl of ice cream. He would get my slippers for me. . . . Random acts of kindness really

belong in relationships. Not only do you make your partner feel good, you feel good, too."

Here are some ideas for random acts of relationship kindness:

- Give hand or foot massages
- Offer a back or shoulder rub
- Listen with complete attention
- Wake up and say, "I'm so happy to see you."
- Call from work, just to say, "I love you and I'm thinking about you."
- Touch your partner; give him or her a hug or a caress
- Give flowers without a special occasion
- Leave a note
- Give a compliment
- Surprise your partner with his or her favorite food
- Run an errand for your partner
- Get up and get snacks during commercials
- Hold your partner in a prolonged hug

Do three random acts of kindness this week and see how your partner responds. Don't focus on "What's in it for me?" Learn to give without conditions, and don't talk about how great you were for being kind. You don't want to say, "Boy was I tired, but I filled your car up with gas because I'm a nice guy." This is getting back to that "tit for tat" attitude that only creates obligation and stress in your relationship. Be kind and then be quiet!

Activity #3: Make a Date to Talk About Your Dreams

When I asked Cal, "What are your dreams for the future? What do you secretly want to do?" his wife Kelly quickly answered, "He wants a big house at the beach."

Kelly was therefore stunned when Cal said, "Actually, I've always wanted to turn the basement into a workshop and make old-fashioned wooden toys."

"What?" Kelly asked. "How come you never told me this before?"

Cal told his wife what many partners tell each other when asked this question: "Because you never asked."

It may be hard to believe, but right now there are millions of people who have known their partners for years and have no idea what their dreams are. But it's important to share our secret wishes and desires.

Make a date with your partner specifically to share dreams. No talk about money or other stressful subjects is allowed. Get a babysitter if you need one. Go to a restaurant or plan a quiet evening at home. (One couple I know find that long walks help them get into the spirit of the exercise.) Wherever you go or whatever you do, really focus on each other. Here are some dos and don'ts to help you get started:

Do:

- Listen with an open mind.
- Ask, "How can I help you make this dream come true?" Donna had always wanted to work with poor children in a Third World country. Because that wasn't realistic at that time in her life, she decided to try volunteering in a shelter for abused women and children. Her husband Stan supported her by giving her encouragement and babysitting their two children.
- Share your dreams from childhood. Often our dreams survive from an early age.
- Share your dreams from time to time to see if they've changed or if there's any way to make them happen.

Don't:

- Judge. This is not your dream. Don't say, "That's ridiculous," or otherwise negatively comment.
- Feel threatened. Your partner may say, "I've always dreamed of living off the land in a small village in Tahiti," but that doesn't mean he wants to pick up and move.
- Try to take charge. When Kelly found out about Cal's dream, she immediately began listing items they would need to get Cal started on building toys. Though her intent

was good, it's not her responsibility to make her husband's dream come true.

Activity #4: Cultivate a Shared Interest

It's perfectly normal and healthy for partners to have different interests. I know many couples who go their separate ways on the weekends or even go on seperate vacations. Ellie liked outdoor adventure trips while Brendan liked to just lie on the beach and relax. For this couple, it made sense to vacation separately or to fly to a location together and then "Do our own thing." There's no law that says you have to do the same things.

But it is rewarding to connect some of the time through a shared interest or hobby. Having a shared interest helps to solidify your identity as a couple. If you do something that you both enjoy and find exciting, it has a synergistic effect. Your individual excitement will spill over and become excitement for each other. Gazing at trees you planted together, a craft you made together, a room you decorated together, or an empty, souvenir bottle of wine from a wine-tasting class you took together can help you center on your identity as a couple. In addition to creating positive memories, the sheer time spent together doing shared activities pulls you away from your competing individual demands.

Steve and Becky had worked with me for several months. Their relationship had been hurt badly by years of underlying toxic thoughts and a lack of mutual appreciation. Through hard work and determination, they learned to detoxify their thinking and to become more mindful of the value of their relationship. They were determined to overcome the Three-D Effect and were eager to try exercises or strategies to put their problems in the past and get close again. I suggested that they reconnect using the strong mutual interest in remodeling that they had enjoyed together in past years. They remodeled their master bathroom, had a great time, and went on a well-deserved, long-neglected vacation with the money they saved by doing it themselves.

Of course, I'm not recommending that you force common interests where there are none. If you like to go antiquing but your partner hates it, or your partner loves to cook elaborate meals but you'd rather have a burger and fries, then don't force it. You can't force your partner to have the same interests as you. What you can do instead is find a whole new activity or hobby you can try together. It doesn't mean you have to do it every week, but you should make time to do a fun activity together once a month. Be open to trying new things. Be willing to stick with it until you find an activity that's fun for both of you. Here are a few suggestions that several of my clients have tried:

Play pool or go bowling
Take a class together
Join a wine-tasting or restaurant club
Play cards or a board game like Scrabble
Join a coed volleyball team
Garden
Try rock climbing
Go bike riding
Take occasional long walks around the neighborhood or go hiking
Join the gym together (one couple I know now works out with a private trainer)
Take a yoga class
Take day trips to historic sites or museums
Attend a lecture
Join a book group for couples
Volunteer together

Activity #5: Stare into Each Other's Eyes

Many times, my clients groan when I suggest this one. When they try it, a lot of couples laugh, but after a while, they see why it's so powerful and how it works. Try it and you'll see what I mean.

Sit facing one another with your eyes closed. Take some slow, deep breaths to quiet your mind. Visualize something pleasant and relaxing, like walking on the beach. Allow yourself to relax and just sit this way for a few minutes—many people rush it at first, because they're uncomfortable or nervous. When you're ready, open your eyes and look into your partner's eyes. (No talking!) Look past your partner's face and personality. What you want to see is the window into his or her soul. Now ask yourself:

- What it is about the person in front of you that touches your heart the most?
- What qualities attracted you to this person in the first place, and allowed you to fall in love?
- What gifts are you receiving from this person?
- How has this relationship enriched your life?

Use these questions to get in touch with your deepest feelings of love and appreciation.

Whichever of you is now ready can put these thoughts and feelings into words. Just let the words flow from you without editing them. Be emotional. Be poetic. This can be hard at first, but it will get easier each time. Be courageous in your vulnerability. Practice expressing thoughts and feelings about your partner that you have never expressed before. Take turns speaking.

On a piece of paper, write down the positive thoughts you have reawakened about your partner. Here is what Scott wrote about his wife Jean:

Scott: "When I looked into Jean's eyes, I started to crack up. But I stayed with it. Then, while looking at her, I felt a chill. It was kind of weird at first, but I felt warm waves of positive feelings come over me. I felt humbled. Humbled by how much this woman—my wife—loves me. I got in touch with what an honor it is to have someone who loves me that much. This can be a lonely world and at times I feel invisible in it—but not when I'm around Jean. In the midst of staring into her eyes, I felt grateful for Jean's loyalty to me and how much she believes in me."

Activity #6: Tune in to Comedy Central

Humor is one of the most powerful bridges between people. Sharing a joke can be a highly fun yet intimate experience. Laughing makes us feel good. Laugh with your partner as often as you can.

Reminiscing about funny, goofy times can feel really good as a couple. The following exercise is suggested to help you connect or reconnect through laughter. Sit down together and separately write down some of the funniest things that happened throughout your history as a couple. Choose the one or two most humorous ones and share your memories.

Stuart and Holly did this exercise and here's what they came up with:

Holly: "I remember when we had just picked up our used Volvo station wagon from the dealership. You thought it was such a great car and you were so excited. You playfully yelled at me for putting my feet up on the dash and leaving marks on it. Do you remember what happened next? Remember how we went to celebrate by going through the McDonald's drive-through? As we were coming out of the drive-through, you started to tell me again to keep my feet off the dash and you hit that trash can at the end of the parking lot. Everybody at the picnic tables looked at you and that old lady shook her head. That was so funny!!"

Stuart: "How about the time when you had your brother, Al, came over and you tried to set him up with our neighbor at the time; I think her name was Rachel. When they met in our living room he was very polite to her. But remember when she got up and excused herself to use the bathroom? Remember your brother's snarls and growls at you because he had absolutely no interest in her at all? Later that night you kept trying to sell him on her personality and he was just not hearing it. I was cracking up."

Activity #7: Be a Charity Case

Doing something that you don't like for your partner makes a huge positive statement. It also helps to enrich your relationship. By putting your partner's needs ahead of yours, you are demonstrating consideration and thoughtfulness. This helps your partner to feel cared about and important. So pick an activity that your partner enjoys, but you don't like. Maybe he likes watching the Sunday football games.

Okay, so maybe you really dread a Sunday of sports, but he really loves them. So watch a game with him. Engross yourself in the frenzy of the fans, the choreography of the cheerleaders' dance routines, or the joy your partner gets from being involved.

Or maybe, she likes to dance—a lot, and you really don't like to dance at all. Suck it up. Do it for her. Even though you don't like dancing, go out to the club and amuse yourself by learning new dance moves. Just do the best you can and have fun.

When Carly asked if she could go fishing with her longtime partner Greg, he was stunned. "I always say, 'Do you want to come?' and she would always make a sarcastic comment about how she would rather go to the dentist or something like that. So when she said, 'Yes, I would like to come,' I didn't know what to do. I thought she would complain the whole time. I was having toxic thoughts about how she would ruin the day. But she was a real trooper. I saw a side of Carly that day that I haven't seen in years—kind of like when you first meet someone and start to get to know them. I hope she'll come again."

Activity #8: Play a Head Game

No, not the toxic, Head Gambling kind. What I mean is play a constructive game to help rediscover and learn new things about each other. Go to the store and buy a deck of 3" x 5" index cards. Write down questions for each other (one question per card) and take turns asking them. There are no rules here except respect and emotional safety. So make answering questions optional and don't comment or criticize any responses from one another. Give it a whirl.

Below are a list of questions and items you can put on separate cards to get you started. Feel free to add as many of your own as you like to create a deck of cards you can use over and over.

- What is your earliest childhood memory?
- What are you most proud of having done?
- If you could spend a day doing anything you wanted, what would you do?

- If you could be anyone in the world for a day, who would you want to be?
- What gives you the most peace and serenity?
- Comment on your need for space.
- Comment on your need for privacy.
- What is your favorite movie of all time and why?
- If you were to be described as an animal, which one would it be?
- What do you like least and most about your in-laws (if applicable)?
- What do you keep telling your mate that he or she just does not get?
- What is your biggest regret?
- Comment on your need for intellectual stimulation.
- What is your favorite time of day?

Activity #9: It's Time to Make Time

Toxic thoughts and a lack of relationship mindfulness can really pave the way for the Three-D Effect. By now you have lots of tools to help you in those areas. Yet, there is also one simple truth that is important to keep in mind. If you don't make an effort to spend time together, your relationship will start to deteriorate. Many couples feel that it is unromantic to have to use their datebooks to plan time together alongside other important appointments and staff meetings. Nothing could be farther from reality. Grab your appointment books, sit down together, and schedule lunches, dinners, and getaways. Your relationship deserves this level of priority.

Don't get discouraged if your partner does not jump to make this happen. I think of Jeanette who impressed me very much with her "take the bull by the horns" approach to planning time with her husband Ivan. She empowered herself by keeping mindful of the fun they have when they are together. Rather than doing nothing because Ivan gets caught up with his busy work life, Jeanette scheduled a bimonthly overnight at a bed and breakfast or nice hotel on a regular basis. Ivan loved and appreciated it.

Activity #10: Do Nothing at All

I remember being on vacation some years ago and meeting a couple. The resort was absolutely beautiful, the water in the pool was glistening and you could hear the soothing waves of the ocean nearby. Yet, I heard the partners complaining that they were bored. "There's nothing to do here," they complained.

I felt sorry for them. You don't always have to be doing *something* to make worthwhile use of your time. But in our "get up and go" culture, with so much stimulation and hustle and bustle, it's easy to forget this. Whether it is a tropical island or your own backyard, you can enjoy each other's company by just lounging around. So even if you appear to be doing nothing at all, that's okay. Being able to relax in each other's company—without the television or radio blaring in the background—makes a positive statement about your relationship. It says that you are comfortable being together.

Roberta and Gina, a long-term couple, discovered that underneath their desire to always be doing something together—taking weekend trips, antiquing, dancing, going to the theater, going whitewater rafting, and attending yoga classes—was the fear that if they slowed down or stopped their flurry of activity, they would discover that their relationship was dull or flat.

They discovered their fear when I suggested that instead of running around all weekend, they spend some quiet time alone. During the session Gina revealed that she was tired of all the hustle and bustle. When Roberta asked, "Why didn't you tell me?" Gina replied that she was afraid that Roberta would be bored and feel unfulfilled just hanging out with her. In other words, she was jumping to Catastrophic Conclusions about her relationship.

Interestingly, Gina also shared that she had an emotional ghost coming into play. She told Roberta how busying herself in activities helped her during her teen years, when she felt a sense of conflict and shame about her sexual orientation. Her solution to deal with these feelings, and to avoid being "found out" by her parents, was to run from one activity to another. By keeping so busy, Gina was able to sidestep the inevitable questions about dating boys from her parents. While Gina later embraced her sexual orientation (and her parents were supportive of her), Gina's ghost was the sense that safety meant constantly being busy. Fortunately for Gina, and for Roberta, Gina's ability to look at this pattern was a huge step forward in her relationship with Roberta.

The fear of slowing down is very common for couples. I see this a lot in couples with kids who are growing up and need their mother and father's attention. As Lisa, a mother of two boys, put it, "You get so used to connecting over the kids, you forget how to connect about anything else." This is why it can be so great to spend time alone together. You will remember how to connect.

Activity #11: Make the Little Things Count

Couples often fall into the trap of becoming "ships passing in the night." Make your interactions count, no matter how brief and small. A smile when passing your partner in the hallway can go a long way to feeling connected. A quick joke or pat on the shoulder also feels good. Stopping to ask, "How was your day?" and *really* listening to the answer can make your partner feel very valued and special. And, you have to admit that making the little things count is pretty simple.

Cherish the moments and be mindful of how valuable they are. Kristen and Alex found that making the most out of their brief interactions mattered even more after the kids were born. Kristen said, "We just got into a pattern where we were like robots. You can get so caught up that you forget how joyful it is to connect in a small but meaningful way."

TO SUM IT ALL UP

THESE ACTIVITIES ARE just a few of the many ways that you can strengthen your intimate connection with your partner. Use them. They will go a long way toward helping you and your partner reach a better place in your relationship. In addition, look for Web sites for couples, go to bookstores and look at the self-help sections, and look for activities through community and religious organizations. Yes, relationships take work. But what doesn't? Your car needs maintenance, your house needs maintenance, and so does your relationship.

11

At Last,
Real Romance!

IF YOU NEED one last good rea-
son to keep your relationship free of toxic thinking, here it is: Once
you are detoxified, you will finally be free to pursue real romance in
your relationship. I want you to finish this book feeling inspired to
find, keep, and cherish real romance.

But what exactly is real romance? If only the Hollywood version
of romance was real. We could all glide into euphoric relationships,
rescued from the singles scene. And of course, we really would be
able to read each other's minds, complete each other's sentences, and
be transformed.

But that's not the way the real world works. So let's get over it and
get on with finding real romance. And don't worry, just because you
can't read each other's minds doesn't mean you can't feel the power of
romance and even get swept away by it at times. And don't think that

just because you can't have the Hollywood version of romance, your version won't be exciting, passionate, and a whole lot of fun. It will be!

You must begin your pursuit of real romance by understanding that romance is a choice. Romance is an attitude. Romance is a commitment to a healthy relationship. And, surprise, romance often has nothing to do with sex. In fact, let's separate the two right now. Romance is based on positive emotions, while sex, in the technical sense, is based on movements and physical sensations. I view sexual contact as an honor, a gift of sharing pleasures with someone else. Unfortunately, sex is not always viewed this way, particularly by young people who are experimenting with it. With sex it is important to realize that what feels good is not always good for you. Sex can feel good, but without an emotional connection, sex also can feel empty.

THE SECRET TO ROMANCE, REVEALED

YES, ROMANCE ENCOMPASSES sexual relations, but it is much more than that. Romance is an expression of love and is all about forming an emotional connection. But emotional connections don't just maintain themselves—you need to nurture them. That's it. That's the big secret to finding and keeping real romance alive in your partnership. It's not about being good looking or buying expensive gifts; it's about making the commitment to do the work to keep the emotional connection between you and your partner alive. Romance happens by making your relationship a priority.

We've got to work at romance because living in our fast-paced, demanding culture adds stress to relationships. After the initial love buzz wears off—after the honeymoon phase is over—romance is not automatic. Distractions like children and work responsibilities can squeeze any feeling of romance out of you. Lingering disagreements resulting in toxic thoughts can cause tensions to rise. Sometimes we just get too busy to deal with the little irritations. Disappointment over what our mates fail to do chills romance. I know it can be tough when you're busy and tired and constantly being interrupted to remember to keep the spark in your relationship alive. Therefore, it's important to take a few minutes every now and then to just think about romance and its importance to your relationship.

FIFTEEN KEYS TO FINDING AND KEEPING REAL ROMANCE IN YOUR RELATIONSHIP

AS YOU'LL SOON see, these fifteen keys for nurturing romance require effort, but they will not wear you out. You won't feel tired or clueless—in fact, you will feel just the opposite.

#1: Keep Your MAP Handy

Your good old MAP (Mindfulness, Alternatives, and Practice) model is your first key to keeping your romance alive. Mindfulness keeps you aware of your partner's value as someone with whom you share the honor of intimacy. Mindfulness similarly helps you to keep the value of your relationship alive. Since romance is about valuing one another, it makes sense that mindfulness is a key foundation that romance is built upon.

Alternatives are your toxic thought zappers. Alternatives are what you use to challenge and dispute those relationship-damaging toxic thoughts. They are the guided missiles that blast your toxic thoughts to bits. Whether you are disarming *Should* Bombs, trading in your All or Nothing thoughts for more reasonable ones, or calming down that Overactive Imagination, alternatives are a crucial tool to help you repair relationship breakdowns. Alternatives are what you need to control your thoughts and emotions, communicate effectively, and address conflicts—and they are also important contributors to romance. Think about it; do you feel like doing something thoughtful for your partner when you're full of toxic thoughts toward him or her?

Practice is about the determination and commitment needed to keep your relationship working over the long haul. In a world that is increasingly fast-paced and complex, nothing is more romantic than an enduring commitment to your partner.

I bet you never thought of your listening skills as a requirement for romance, but that's exactly what they are. Listening is important to the heart and soul of any relationship, and particularly intimate relationships. *Really* listening to your partner helps her or him to feel special. It is a gift and an honor. Intimacy and romance are about feeling special. Being listened to, *really* listened to, feels very good. In order to really listen, it's important to give your partner your undivided attention. I must say that men, in general, seem to have a harder time doing this than women. Men are often compelled to try to do two things at once. His partner will be pouring her heart out and there he is, checking his e-mail, emptying the dishwasher, or even balancing the checkbook. Men do this because they, in general, appear be less comfortable expressing and responding to emotions than women. Many men have been in my office pleading to their partners or me to "Tell me what to do" in the face of their partner's negative emotions. Men traditionally have been socialized into being the "fixers" and problem-solvers. Emotions are more abstract to most men, and many become frustrated when they can't fix their partner's emotions.

I remember how Randall looked lost and frustrated when he told me he didn't know what to do as he sat in front of his tearful wife, Francine. Francine felt deeply betrayed by her parents, who had given the exclusive of use of the family shore house to her younger sister.

Randall asked, "You're telling me all she wants me to do is listen?"

Francine responded, "Yes, Randall, but I mean listen without doing something when I talk and listen without telling me what to do. . . . You *never* listen to me."

I smiled and gently said, "Never?"

Francine grimaced and then smiled and said, "Well, I guess not never, but I do feel that it is so hard for Randall to sometimes really listen to me the way I'd like him to."

So, for the remainder of the session, I had Randall sit on his hands (so he would not fiddle with things) and hold eye contact with Francine. Randall, a good-natured guy, even volunteered to have me put a piece of tape over his mouth to keep him from jumping in to try to solve the problem, which I promptly did. And Randall listened, really listened. Randall quickly learned that really listening was work—and it was also the most rewarding gift he had ever given to Francine.

Of course, women also have listening issues, but judging by the number of women who complain about this to me, men need to pay special attention to listening with total focus. It's annoying to try to talk to your partner when you sense he or she's emotionally ten miles away. This can really drain the romance out of the relationship. With more dual-career marriages and relationships, and the additional competing demands for our attention and time, such as e-mail, voice mail, and children's activities, it is becoming more important than ever to dedicate your sincere attention to your intimate partner. No one has yet to show up in my office and say, "The reason my relationship is in a crisis is because my husband or wife listens to me too much." (Please review the empathetic listening exercise on page 142 for more practice.)

#3: Be Honest

Relationships that are not built on honesty are at risk for problems, including problems with romance. I'm not saying that you have to share every thought—toxic or not—with your partner. In fact, the strategies I have provided in earlier chapters emphasize that you dispute toxic thoughts within the privacy of your own mind. But, your basic needs and desires make up who you are as a person. To keep important issues or feelings from your partner is deceptive and can be downright cruel.

It's okay to be confused. It is okay to have mixed feelings about some things, like how you feel about your partner's new job, which requires travel or new friends. This will happen from time to time, but, again, it's important to work toward honesty with your partner. If you don't, your romantic relationship will suffer.

Take Julian. He was not ready to marry Rosie, but he felt scared to tell her. Giving in to her wishes rather than risking losing her, Julian agreed to a wedding date, yet he was not comfortable making this commitment at that point in the relationship. As the wedding date got closer, Julian experienced considerable anxiety and angst.

Romance was the last thing on his mind and the couple's sex life came to a screeching halt two months before the wedding date. Rosie, not understanding what was happening, became convinced that Julian didn't love her anymore and wasn't attracted to her so she called off the wedding.

Tory and Matt also found out the hard way about dishonesty's ability to diminish romance. When they first met, Tory didn't want to "rock the boat," so she pretended that Matt's passion for golf every Sunday didn't bother her. In reality, not only did it bother her, she resented it (*He should know that I need some time on the weekend too!*)

When Tory began to complain about Matt's golfing, Matt resented this, claiming that Tory had been very supportive of his golf from the beginning. Soon enough, Tory stopped doing nice things for him and Matt stopped doing nice little things for her. They stopped caring whether or not they had dinner together every evening, and forget date night. Why bother? They would just end up arguing anyway.

As these two couples show us, honesty greatly impacts romance in relationships. A close friend and colleague of mine puts it very concisely: Secrets kill. Hidden agendas and secrets are like cancers eating away the emotional safety in relationships. It is hard to feel romantic when you don't feel safe.

I remember Chip, who was petrified to tell his wife Gloria about a large sum of money he had lost on an investment he made without her knowledge. Chip had come in to see me with "out of the blue" panic attacks. Once he disclosed to me his deception to Gloria, he agreed that he needed to come clean with her. Gloria was hurt and angry with Chip, but she also felt relieved.

Gloria: "I just knew something was up the last few months. Chip was acting weird. I kept asking him what was the matter and he kept saying, 'nothing.' It drove me nuts because I knew there was something going on."

Chip and Gloria worked things out. They learned that though deception may seem easier, in the long run it only creates more problems and anxiety for both partners.

While being honest about what you really want and need is very important, it's also very important to realize that not all of those wants and needs will be fulfilled. It is simply not realistic to think that one person can give you everything you will ever want and need.

You may laugh at how painfully obvious this sounds, but I have had many a client cry in my office feeling unfulfilled. I don't mean unfulfilled in the huge ways, such as having a partner who cheats. It's usually far less significant than that. Like Janelle, who felt that Dennis *should not* be so overly involved with coaching their son's soccer team. "He is just *never* around during soccer season and this is going to get worse every year," she said with disdain. "He *should* know how alone I feel."

My first order of business was to help Janelle get rid of her toxic thoughts.

We conquered her All or Nothing thinking ("never"), *Should Bomb* ("should know"), and Catastrophic Conclusion ("it will get worse every year"). By getting rid of her toxic thoughts, Janelle was able to see how many of her needs were being met: Dennis was affectionate and a good provider, and his dedication to their son also helped Janelle feel good about the family. Janelle reframed the time demands of soccer season as "inconvenient" for her, but this did not mean her marriage or family were in jeopardy. Janelle ended up understanding that love was not always about getting what she wanted. I'm happy to add that, somewhat mysteriously, once Janelle lightened up on Dennis, he seemed to find more time to be with her. Isn't it funny how things sometimes work out that way—out of the blue?

Don't go toxic and get sucked into the Blame Game or Disillusionment Doom, or any other toxic thoughts just because your partner is not handing you all your wants and desires on a silver platter. Focus on giving your partner all *you* can (outside of inappropriately enabling serious problems associated with serious mental illness, verbal or physical abuse, or active, destructive addictions). The more you put in, the more you will get back.

Fun . . . isn't that what you thought love was all about? Early days of romance filled with lots of highs and no lows. You understandably wished, and maybe even fooled yourself into expecting, that the initial euphoria of infatuation would go on forever. Yet once the realities of work responsibilities, bills, demands on your time, housework, and demands from others take their toll, you may literally forget to laugh and have fun with your partner. So many couples complain to me that they don't have fun anymore. "We don't laugh together the way we used to," they say.

So I tell these couples, "Do fun things again. Make each other laugh."

Yes, this is an obvious answer, but if you're not having fun, you do need to make an effort to lighten up and start trying to have fun again. Many couples get apathetic about infusing their relationships with joy and laughter. It's easy to let this happen; you get stressed out from work and the kids and grocery shopping and the next thing you know, you've lost your sense of humor and fun. You now have "issues" in the relationship, and that also drains the fun out of it.

But laughter is a potent love medicine. Laughter is an intimacy-builder for couples. It feels good to laugh and let go. Laughter can go a long way in helping you resolve your issues, like it did for Abe and Lydia, who were having issues with their fourteen-year-old daughter, Elaine. Elaine's teen rebellion was taking a toll on their marriage. Abe often lost his temper with Elaine, especially when she wore what he thought were skimpy outfits or played her heavy metal music too loudly. Lydia was caught in the middle and resented Abe for "losing it," since he was the adult.

> Lydia: "Our house was so depressing. It was like we were all sneaking around trying not to notice each other and get in another big fight. Abe resented me for not supporting him more. Elaine resented me for not supporting her more. I was really starting to get worn down from all of this. Abe and I hadn't connected in months.

"One night when Elaine and I got home from the mall, we found Abe dressed in the most ridiculous outfit—tight jeans and a cutoff T-shirt. He even had high heels on. He started dancing like a wild man around the kitchen to Elaine's favorite music from one of her CDs. We all cracked up. This really cut the tension. It was not a complete fix, but it helped. Not only did Elaine feel like she could finally talk to Abe, I felt much more able to connect with him after that, too. We had forgotten how to laugh and have fun, both as a family and as a couple."

Some couples make the mistake of trying to recapture the initial feelings of infatuation, which may be long gone (and that's normal). But know that your deeper, more enduring love and appreciation for each other can still be fun. So dance around the kitchen like Abe. Watch funny movies together. Get playful and silly. Start a water fight with the hose. Chase after each other. Tell corny jokes. And most importantly—smile. Smile your way to intimacy and romance.

#6: Find Time to Be Together Every Day

Fred and Dana were in my office, complaining that they had little time to spend together. The parents of two young children and a dual-career couple (along with Dana attending a night school), they did not have much time to spare.

Dana just wanted a little alone time with Fred every day. Fred felt that usually meant they had to go to a nice restaurant, and with Dana in school, money was tight. Dana told Fred she could care less if it was just the two of them hanging out in a booth at the nearby fast food restaurant. The point Dana made to Fred was that they just needed time to be together—it did not matter where.

Take Dana's advice. Whether you splurge on a vacation for just the two of you, walk around your yard, go for a picnic in the park, work out together, visit a library or bookstore, or howl at the moon together, just be together. Try new things together as well. Take a tennis class or a wine-tasting class. Just make it a priority to be together.

#7: Choose Your Battles

You've heard the expression "Life is short." It's true. So why waste your time on needless conflicts? I am excited that you can now know how to internally dispute your toxic thinking toward your partner. I am excited about how you will find that rethinking your toxic thoughts with reasonable alternatives will take you light-years ahead in bringing harmony and satisfaction to your relationship. Also, being mindful about the value of your relationship and your partner is very important to keeping romance alive.

Use the techniques I have shown you in this book and there will be far fewer battles. If you must fight, follow the eight rules for fighting fair, which I describe in Chapter Nine. Keep in mind, nothing squashes romance more than needless battles and unfair argument behaviors, like yelling, door slamming, and name-calling. They are a sure road to the Three-D Effect. Real, enduring romance comes from accepting your partner for who he or she is, and not dwelling on what he or she is not. Stop insisting that your partner change. Stop being overly critical. Lighten up. So what if she never shuts the kitchen cabinets and he never takes the garbage out on time? The world won't end. Be supportive and empathetic; your partner will respond more positively and make more adjustments for you, and there will be far fewer battles.

#8: Be Polite

Being polite is an important yet sorely neglected key to romance. Being polite is also about treating your partner with respect. It amazes me how some individuals treat delivery people and deli clerks with more kindness and respect than they treat their own intimate partners. Usually, when we slack off on our manners, it's the people closest to us who suffer. As simple as it sounds, if you want to be romantic, be polite to your partner. Here are some simple ways to be polite that are important in a romantic relationship:

- Say "please" and "thank you."
- Ask "How was your day?"

- Listen without interrupting.
- Remain mindful of your social graces, like not chewing with your mouth open or forgetting to put your napkin on your lap.
- Introduce your partner to others when in a group. Make him or her feel included in the conversation.
- Hold the door for each other.

Many couples that I have worked with are amazed at how much closer they feel when they remember to be polite to one another. It's like saying, "I value you. I value this relationship."

It works. Try it!

#9: Act "As If"

William James (1842–1910), considered by many to be the father of psychology, spoke these famous words, "Act as if what you do makes a difference. It does." I want you to apply this to your romance. When you act romanticly, you are romantic. When you act considerately, you are considerate. When you act attentively, you are attentive. Now I'm not saying that you should be smiling when inside you are fuming, and that you should make a practice of faking your real feelings. What I am saying is that to give the romance in your relationship a jump start, it all begins with your actions. Don't wait for your partner to act "as if" first. Don't wait until you have that warm and fuzzy feeling in your stomach again—it may be a long time in coming unless someone takes some action.

Take the initiative. Start with gentle hand-holding, a light squeeze on the shoulder, a hug, or a light kiss on the lips. Go slow and go steady. Just make up your mind that if you *act as if* you are more loving and romantic, your relationship will *be* more loving and romantic.

#10: Spend Time Apart to Enjoy Being Together

"Absence makes the heart grow fonder."

I believe that to some extent this is really true. While individuals and couples vary in their needs for physical and psychological space apart from one another, it is a solid recommendation for you and your partner to take time and space for yourselves. Being your own person helps you to be more complete and developed. The more whole you are as separate people, the more you offer to one another as a couple. So pursue your separate interests and use this time to recenter and rejuvenate your energy and spirit—which you then bring back to your partner.

When Anthony enrolled in a personal growth workshop in another city for a long weekend, Laurie, his wife of twelve years, was at first "annoyed and suspicious."

Laurie: "I thought, *Well, this is how it starts. This is how a man starts leaving you, in long weekends first and then separate vacations, and after that it's divorce city.* But in confronting my toxic thoughts I had to admit that Anthony had never given me a reason to doubt my trust. After a lot of talking and soul-searching, I knew that I had to support Anthony's decision to go. It was a long weekend for me, alone at home with our two girls, but I acted cheerful when he called.

"When he got home, Anthony was like a new man. He was energized, excited, and in a bubbly sort of good mood. For the first time in a long time, he couldn't wait to share his life with me. We sat up late that night and talked and talked. We held hands and cuddled like we did when we dated. He told me that he thought about me and the girls the whole time. It just made him realize how much he loves his life with us.

"His trip inspired me to do something like that for myself. I'm going on my own long weekend. It's for a career-building seminar, and I'm very excited about going and then being able to share the experience with my husband the way he shared his with me."

#11: Know Size Does Not Matter

Consider that little things count for a lot in romance. You really can do little things that mean so much. Tuck a love note in a lunch bag or on the passenger seat of the car when you know your loved one will be going out. Send flowers to work, send a card in the mail, or call him on the phone just to say, "I love you." It's not just about being supportive during hard times, it's about doing the little things—buying socks when he needs them, making her dinner when she works late—that show you're thinking of your partner. The gifts don't have to be expensive. Make cookies or buy that paperback she's been wanting to read. Make pancakes on Saturday morning or make a collage of photos of just the two of you.

When you take care of the little things, the bigger things get a lot easier, too.

#12: Flirt with the One You Really Love

Most of us think that we can turnoff our smoldering glances and lingering touches directed at others as soon as we commit to a relationship. We couldn't be more wrong. Flirting shows that you're still attracted to your partner and can combat that completely unsexy predictability. Below is a list of five ways to flirt with the one you love:

1. Pretend you are meeting for the first time in a public place.
3. Pretend you are meeting for the first time in your bedroom.
4. Put on fresh lipstick and kiss a 3" x 5" index card—put the imprint in the driver's seat of your partner's car. Guys, you can leave a rose on your partner's driver's seat or a card expressing your love.
5. Smile—seductively!
6. Send your partner a spicy letter in the mail or by e-mail (if you're sure that no one else will see it).

#13: Look Good

Though it's important to deal with Disillusionment Doom, like *I didn't know she'd be this big after childbirth*, or *Oh my God, he's growing hair in his ears!*, it's also important to keep yourself attractive to your partner. None of us is perfect. Don't try to be. You don't have to be a supermodel or ready for the cover of *GQ* or *Glamour* magazine, but do try to be the best that you can be. Watch what you eat. Exercise. Dress nicely. Keep up with good personal hygiene. Feeling good about how you look will keep your partner inspired to do the same. The more attractive you each feel, the more romantic you will each feel.

Nina: "No, you're not going to see me in a bikini anytime soon, not after having our second child six months ago, but that doesn't mean I don't watch the details. It's easy to let yourself go when you're at home all day with the kids and getting spit up on. But I make a point of keeping my hair styled, wearing sexy underwear (at least on the bottom—right now I'm still in my nursing bra), and keeping my legs and underarms shaved. I've made a rule that I don't wear sweat suits anymore. I do think it makes a difference in how John sees me and how I see myself. I don't feel perfect, but I feel attractive."

John: "I really appreciate that Nina takes the time to look nice for me and for herself. It makes me go the extra mile, too. I try to lift weights and work out on the treadmill at least four times a week. I make a point of shaving, even on the weekends, because Nina gets turned off when I get scruffy. I think we are more romantic with each other because we are both taking care of ourselves and because we're both making the effort."

#14: Stop Just Thinking About Sex—Talk About it, Too

I know I said that romance does not necessarily have anything to do with sex. But sex does count—a lot. Sex is something we all think about. It's part of our daily lives in some way or another, and an important part of our relationships. Sex is the physical act that you only experience with your partner, and that's a special thing.

However, despite all we hear, read, see, and think about sex, it's the one topic that many of us find difficult to talk about with our partners. We may be quite good at expressing our deepest thoughts and feelings on other aspects of our lives, but when it comes to the topic of sex, many of us are silent. Remember that open and honest communication doesn't stop when the bedroom door closes. Being able to talk about your desires, fantasies, needs, limits, and even insecurities about sex is critical to not only improving your sex life, but dealing with your fears and apprehensions.

Here are some guidelines for discussing sex with your partner:

- Be able to laugh at yourself. Stop taking yourself so seriously when it comes to sex, and remember that this is just a natural part of life. Few of us look perfect naked. We all jiggle, make strange sounds, emit odors, and bump our heads from time to time—it's nothing to feel embarrassed about, and neither is talking about sex.
- Never laugh at your partner. Couples need to be in an emotional safety zone when talking about sex, especially when sharing fantasies. This isn't going to happen if you treat your partner like he or she is strange or somehow inappropriate for having a fantasy. Some people laugh when they're nervous—be mindful not to laugh when talking about sex if you have this habit.
- Trade fantasies or desires about sex. One way to get the conversation rolling is for each of you to take a turn confessing a secret fantasy or desire, with the premise that you're only sharing. That way, if there's something you can't see yourself doing, you're not put on the spot. What this does is to get things out in the open, which can often lead to a dialogue.
- Don't expect your partner to be enthusiastic about every desire or fantasy you have—you're probably not going to be crazy about all of his or hers, either. The key is to share these things openly, and to be secure enough in ourselves and our relationships to laugh at ourselves. Let's face it, your partner has seen you at your best and your worst, and you count on him or her to be understanding and supportive. Sex should be no different.
- Put the sex education manuals away. At least put them away until you are *really* ready to use them. It amuses me how often partners, more often men than women, will order sex manual when their partner's have not talked to them for a week. The best and hottest foreplay is truly talking, listening to one another, and treating each other

with respect. Couples lost in The Three-D Effect will not find long-term solutions to their problems through torrid, hot sex. It is feeling emotionally connected that really makes for full, long-lasting romance and intimacy.

It may not be easy at first, but the more you openly discuss matters of sex with your partner, the easier and more natural this will become. You can't expect your partner to be enthusiastic about every one of your whims and fantasies. So be accepting and have mutual respect; this attitude leads to a mutually satisfying sex life.

A healthy sex life is important to every relationship, and a good place to begin is through open and honest communication. Knowing the other's needs, desires, and limits is critical, and this can't be accomplished if you stop talking when the bedroom door closes.

#15: Know How Easy It Is to Take Your Relationship for Granted

The "eleventh-hour couples," as I refer to those who come to see me when they are on the brink of divorce, all seem to share one common denominator: They make proclamations such as "He never appreciated me" and "She's never showed me that she really cared about me."

These perceptions may have begun as distorted, toxic thoughts, but they became deeply ingrained beliefs. Years and years of a lack of mindfulness of the value of the relationship, combined with too many unchallenged toxic thoughts, can leave couples drained, demoralized, and ready to call it quits. You can detoxify all you want. You can smoke out all of your unreasonable, unfair toxic thoughts, but if you take your relationship for granted, your hard work won't help.

It's common for one partner to feel like he or she is "done" with the relationship, and the other comes begging for another chance. Too often, the response is "Sorry, but it's too little, too late." Of course, unless the party "wanting out" looks at his or her role in the relationship instead of just seeing him- or herself as a victim, he or she is likely to repeat some of the issues in the next relationship.

Avoid this mess by practicing ongoing appreciation. Over time, couples may forget about one of romance's basic rules: Express regular praise in a loving manner and keep criticism to a minimum. Not just thinking about but telling your partner the things you admire in him will convey the all-important message "I don't take this relationship for granted."

So find a few minutes of quiet during the day, or at night before falling asleep, to sit or lie quietly together and comment on three things about each of you that pleases the other. While it's easy to compliment physical appearance, give it some thought and show additional consideration by focusing on his or her behavior and character traits. Let your partner know you've noticed the special things he or she has said or done. Perhaps he or she will want to reciprocate immediately afterward, or the next time. Be sure to state your compliments in a positive light, and accept them graciously when you're on the receiving end. This means acknowledging the praise with a simple "thank you," a nod of appreciation, or a gentle kiss. Never downplay what you are being praised for with a comment like "Ah, it was really nothing." Not only will your partner find listening to you easy and bask in the warmth of your appreciation, but your comments will also remind you of your own good qualities.

TO SUM IT ALL UP

ROMANCE IS A state of mind—once you are free of toxic thinking, that is. When you think toxically, you block your good intentions toward your partner and you can feel too drained for the challenge of creating romance. We all have unrealistic expectations of being swept away in ecstasy, and then we're disappointed when we don't feel that way. We don't feel playful or kind—two essential ingredients of romance.

But now that you are on your way to overcoming toxic thoughts, you can find true romance. Mindfulness of your relationship's value, your partner's value, and what an honor it is to be in an intimate relationship are very important. Above all, ongoing mutual respect and appreciation is the key to romance.

CONCLUSION

I SAID AT the beginning of this book that relationships are not easy. I wasn't kidding, was I? But it's my hope that, using the tools and information in this book, your relationship will become considerably easier (though it may never be easy) and significantly more satisfying.

Your relationship is a journey with lots of pitfalls and lots of rewards. Most excitingly, you have a tremendous influence on the quality and fate of your relationship. You really do. By reading this book you have learned how to control your thoughts and feelings toward your intimate partner. By taking responsibility to control your thoughts and feelings, you will realize that, more than you ever could have imagined, your relationship satisfaction begins and ends with you. Be empowered by that revelation.

Here are a few more points to keep in your mind as you work on making your relationship wonderful and lasting:

Practice the principles I have shared about being mindful and detoxifying your thinking. Take responsibility for your emotional ghosts and, if they still haunt you, find the courage to deal with them.

Be empathetic. It will help you avoid toxic thinking and disagreements. When you do fight, fight fairly. Always forgive. You are only human, and so is your partner. Humans, even when they're trying really hard, make mistakes.

Take an active role in enhancing and maintaining your love for your partner. Enjoy the positive changes in your relationship as you follow the strategies I have outlined for you in this book.

You don't have to be passive toward the forces of love. You can take control of your relationship and make your love stronger. You have the power to choose to answer "Yes" to the question "Can this relationship be happier, better, stronger, and longer-lasting?"

Reach down inside and give the best of yourself to your partner. Be grateful for all that he or she gives to you. Focus on what you have and appreciate all of it. Stop worrying about or dwelling on all the "happy couples" around you who seem to effortlessly have an easier time or who are happier than you (it's not easier and they're not happier). While we're making comparisons, discard the scorecards—they'll only make your relationship harder. Trust the goodness in yourself and trust the goodness in your partner. Switch over from autopilot and take an active role in setting the course of the journey of your relationship.

I wish you success in finding newly discovered treasures within yourself and your partner as you move forward in your relationship, mindful of the fact that being in an intimate relationship is an honor. Sharing your hopes, dreams, and future with another human being is a very special privilege. Don't make your partner solely responsible for your happiness. Be realistic in your expectations. And above all, treat yourself and your intimate partner with respect. The rewards you will reap are endless.

ACKNOWLEDGMENTS

WE'RE DEEPLY INDEBTED to the groundbreaking work of many pioneers in the field of cognitive therapy—Aaron Beck, M.D., David Burns, M.D., Albert Ellis, Ph.D., and Martin Seligman, Ph.D. Without their insights and inspiration, this book would not have been possible.

Thanks to our wonderful agent Andrea Pedolsky. Your guidance and knowledge made this book possible. Thanks to our editor, the tireless Sue McCloskey at Marlowe & Company, for believing in this project and for all that you have done to support it.